# THE STATE AND THE CHURCH IN A FREE SOCIETY

BY THE SAME AUTHOR

Teaching the Bible, especially in Secondary Schools (*C.U.P.*)

Personal Experience and the Historic Faith (*Epworth*)

Education into Religion (*Nisbet*)

Natural Religion and Christian Theology (*Nisbet*)

How to know your Bible (*Allen and Unwin*)

The School in the Bush: a critical study of Native Education in Africa (*Longmans*)

The School and the Church (*S.C.M.*)

Truth and Certainty (*the Essex Hall Lecture 1954*)

# THE STATE AND THE CHURCH IN A FREE SOCIETY

BY

A. VICTOR MURRAY

*President of Cheshunt College*
*Cambridge*

THE HIBBERT LECTURES, 1957

CAMBRIDGE
AT THE UNIVERSITY PRESS
1958

PUBLISHED BY
THE SYNDICS OF THE CAMBRIDGE UNIVERSITY PRESS

Bentley House: 200 Euston Road, London, N.W. 1
American Branch: 32 East 57th Street, New York 22, N.Y.



*Printed in Great Britain at the University Press, Cambridge*
*(Brooke Crutchley, University Printer)*

TO

THE MEMORY OF

CLEMENT C. J. WEBB

GUIDE, PHILOSOPHER AND FRIEND

*Dicebat Bernardus Carnotensis nos esse quasi nanos gigantium humeris insidentes, ut possimus plura eis et remotiora videre, non utique proprii visus acumine aut eminentia corporis, sed quia in altum subvehimur et extollimur magnitudine gigantea.*

JOHANNIS SARESBERIENSIS METALOGICON
(ed. C. C. J. W.) III, iv.

# CONTENTS

# PREFACE

This book represents an attempt to elucidate the present position of a very ancient problem which is not even confined to Christianity, although it is the Christian aspect which the book has in view.

In present-day practice in the West the relation of Church and State has gradually been changing its character since 'Church' has come to mean much more than a particular institution however powerful, and 'State' has come to mean not so much the Government (which was formerly its sole reference) as the community at large working through its appointed officers. In these circumstances the pattern of the free society which all progressive communities have or ought to have before them is that of the Christian family, a society in which tensions are neither avoided nor exploited but resolved. This seems to me to be the plain reading of Christ's teaching on the fatherhood of God, the implications of which are still far from being accepted by the modern world. The political problem involved is therefore not that of the limits of political obedience, which so much exercised our forefathers in the seventeenth century, as that of the conditions necessary to enable all sorts and conditions of men to live together in unity and peace. It is here that politics merges into religion and that religion expresses itself in political terms.

Of course the old connotations have not passed away all at once nor is their disappearance likely to be very rapid. The Roman Church in this matter stands where it has always stood. It will never willingly agree to share its power with any other, and it continues to discuss 'Church' and 'State' in terms of institutions. It was only as a matter of expediency that the Roman theory came to admit that the State as well as the Church is a *societas perfecta*, a term which in these days has about it a curiously antiquarian flavour. Communism, our latest revival of ancient ways of thought, must of necessity for its own self-justification continue to postulate the old idea of the State as the Government. In this case, as the State is by definition tyrannical and as tyranny must have an object, there is associated with the seventeenth-century theory the myth of a depressed 'proletariat' whose only road to freedom lies in sabotage and revolution.

Nevertheless it is at least arguable that the future rests with neither type of authoritarianism, Catholic or Communist. Ideologies which are passionately attached to logical completeness must in the long run be defeated by human nature. It is a characteristic of the problems of human life and destiny that we cannot know all the answers, and any institution which claims otherwise is very rightly suspect. In a time of disturbance like the present, however, it is a very great comfort for some types of mind to have at hand an institution or a party which is not ashamed to make such claims. Hence there is a drift of the frustrated towards Rome or Moscow.

In such circumstances Protestantism and democracy find themselves to be natural allies, but the effectiveness of that alliance in building up a Christian society depends on certain conditions, the chief of which is a recognition of the real witness of Protestantism today. I doubt if it is to be found in the Reformation period, and to call Luther and Calvin out of their graves to prophesy to this generation is not only to ignore the vast changes in Church and State in the intervening four centuries but also to deny the work of the Spirit in leading men into new truth. The real evil alike of Roman Catholicism and of Communism is that each is judge in its own cause. The position could not be better put than in a little handbook written for Communists which, with rather limping logic and grammar, states: 'It is essential for the student to realise from the outset that Marxism does not claim recognition because it is based on abstract moral principles but because it is true.'[1] Communism is evidently a closed circle, recognizing no authority and no obligations outside itself. And *mutatis mutandis* the same can be said of the Roman Church, for, although it would admit

[1] Emile Burns, *What is Marxism?* (1948), p. 8.

the existence of a higher authority than itself, it is itself the sole interpreter of that higher authority. It is of the essence of Protestantism that it takes an entirely different line. Not only is Christ the head of the Church (which is also the belief of the Roman Church) but the Church itself is conceived as an ideal by which the Church as an institution is continually judged. The difference between the two positions is clearly seen if we examine any of the *causes célèbres* of Roman Catholic modernism, say that of George Tyrrell, or even the different case of the worker priests in France. It was quite clear in these cases that what was at stake was the overruling authority of the Church. Sooner or later it was this that the would-be reformers had to meet, and on this rock they fell to pieces. In cases of a similar kind in Protestantism, say the Robertson Smith case or even the Colenso decision, the reformer was supported by a large section of his fellows within the Church who, as the years passed, were able to turn themselves into a majority.

The weakness of Protestantism—which is also the weakness of democracy—lies in the place wherein also lies its strength. Depending as it does on persuasion and not force, it is characterized by suspense of judgement, not because of lack of conviction but in order to be sure that it can count on the convictions of a sufficient number of people. This induces a certain spirit of agnosticism which cuts the nerve of effort, and while Protestants are making up their mind the Roman Catholics have entered in at once with complete assurance. Similarly with democracy. The totalitarian states can act and strike at once while the democratic states are seeking to be sure of the suffrage of the majority.

There is no way out of this dilemma, and it is indeed part of the cross which lies heavy on such progressive movements. The reason for it lies in its very refusal to be judge in its own cause.

This feature of Protestantism has emerged only in recent years. It was acknowledged in theory in the sixteenth and seventeenth centuries and was almost totally dishonoured in practice. Not the spirit of God, waited for patiently and with complete commitment, but the Bible became an external rule of faith and was made use of as arbitrarily as any papal bull. The priesthood of all believers as it was first propounded is not far removed in spirit from the Marxian view of the proletariat and was as quietly ignored when it became inconvenient. Justification by faith led straight to the antinomianism of the less balanced sectaries and was the cause of numberless divisions and subdivisions. Natural law, although it was much more in line with the Protestant view of things than the Catholic, was entirely thrown overboard and was salvaged by the Roman Church itself. New presbyter became old priest writ large. Democracy has in our time exhibited a similarly wide variation between theory and practice. There will be enough illustrations in this book to indicate that the corruption of the best is the worst.

Yet it is the best, and these corruptions are defects of a quality. We cannot accept Aquinas's position that monarchy is the best defence against tyranny. The real spirit of Protestantism is very much needed in our time, for it supplies the only genuine alternative to authoritarianism whether Roman or Communist and gives the necessary sanction and challenge to democracy. Both are in eclipse for the time being, but eclipses do not last for ever and even totalitarian states have their day and cease to be.

The Hibbert Lectures for 1957 were delivered in the Universities of Sheffield, Southampton and Hull. I have first of all to thank the Trustees for the great honour that they have conferred upon me in appointing me to this lectureship. Particularly would I thank the Rev. H. Stewart Carter, Professor F. J. M. Stratton, and the then Secretary, Dr J. C. Flower. I am also grateful to my kind hosts and hostesses at the three Universities concerned for their gracious hospitality—Professors Jessop and Castle in Hull, Mr Bramley, Dr F. Masina and Mr Ronald Wilson in Sheffield, and the Vice-Chancellor (Dr D. G. James) in Southampton. My thanks are due and gladly paid to my former colleague, the Rev. R. J. Hall, who stood in when I was absent from Cambridge during so much of the month of February.

## PREFACE

For the table on page 122 I am grateful to Mr W. Hagenbuch of Queens' College, Cambridge, University Lecturer in Economics. For the general preparation of the book I am once more indebted to my secretary, Mrs Amy Richardson, and to my wife for checking the proofs.

A.V.M.

CAMBRIDGE
*1 January 1958*

*See, saith he, that thou make all things according to the pattern shewed to thee in the mount*

HEBREWS viii. 5.

*In heaven, methinks, there is laid up a pattern of the good city which he who desires may behold, and beholding, may set his own house in order. But whether it exists or ever will exist on earth is no matter, for the wise man will live after the manner of it, having nothing to do with any other.*

PLATO, *Republic* IX, 592.

*Injustice is impiety.*

MARCUS AURELIUS

CHAPTER I

# A FREE SOCIETY

## I SOCIETY AND HUMAN NATURE

It is a commonplace in the thought of our time that the world is facing a crisis of a kind that has never before been known in history. One of the signs of that crisis is the division of the nations between various forms of authoritarian rule, of which Communism is the most notable, and various forms of democracy in those areas which for want of a better name we call the 'free world'. How free that free world is may be a matter of doubt, for within each of the so-called free countries we meet a growing challenge to liberty from administrative bodies and from industrial organizations.

These outward divisions, moreover, represent, and are sustained by, a climate of opinion which is found on both sides of the Iron Curtain and which is very largely hostile to liberty. Indeed the very term 'a free society' in the title of this book would be completely unacceptable to large numbers of people who are unaffected by any political or ecclesiastical authoritarianism. We are witnessing a flight from freedom not only in political institutions but also in philosophy, in social life and in religion. Mankind is spiritually homeless and the attempt to find a home is so nerve-racking that many are only too glad to drop into the nearest doss-house that can afford them shelter, no matter what may be the name above the door. These hotels of the spirit are very popular and their attraction lies in the fact that everything is laid on. There is no need to accept responsibility, and there are various ways of avoiding it. The philosophers avoid it by limiting their concern to the literal meaning of words, and 'semantics' is the popular substitute for thought. The economists are content with analysis, as if diagnosis were equivalent to treatment. For those who want religion there is every variety of authoritarianism from the fundamentalist sects to the Church of Rome. And with Communist nationalism in mind the words of Simone Weil strike home, that 'revolution, not religion, is the opiate of the masses'.

Nevertheless, I suggest that political and social happiness is to be found only in a free society, that is to say a society which is not dominated by any sectional interest, political, economic, social or ecclesiastical, to the subordination of all else. I have purposely used the phrase 'sectional interest' for I believe that no free society is possible without regard to ultimate spiritual values, but regard for values is a different thing from domination by an institution, even by an institution that professedly stands for those values. Some of the marks of such a free society would be a political structure in which no man is compelled to be an object for the satisfaction of other men's desires, where the law is above the State, where we have an extended franchise, an educated democracy, freedom of speech, worship and movement, full employment, a concern for standards of quality as the basis of a standard of living, and a society which is informed by genuine acceptance of the principle invented but also travestied by the Communists, 'from each according to his ability: to each according to his need'. Tried by such criteria it is clear that Russia is not and has no desire to be a free society. South Africa is not a free society, nor Spain nor the Irish Republic, nor India, for each of these is dominated by a sectional interest of some sort—ideological, racial or ecclesiastical. Indeed it may be doubted if there is a free society anywhere, for it is possible that every country is under the sway of some dominant group; the United States, for instance, controlled by the supporters of private enterprise and Britain by organized and still more by unorganized labour.

The conception, therefore, of a 'free society' is an expression of an ideal in process of slow realization. To accept it requires an act of faith which not everybody is willing to make. Ideals are suspect nowadays, for ever since World War I we have alternated between idealism and materialism and have ended up in disillusionment. The heaven on earth promised by the Bolshevik revolution of 1917 has turned for millions into its hateful opposite. An appeal to the Fifth Amendment to the American Constitution, intended by the Fathers of 1791 to be a safeguard of liberty, has turned out to be almost a confession of treason. The League of Nations and the United Nations have both made the justice of a war depend entirely upon procedure and they have both been helpless in the face of an aggressor who ignored the rules of the game. The gift of freedom to the South African Boers after the war of 1899–1901 has in the long run been made use of to enslave their black fellow-countrymen under the forms of law. The happy condition of a free Ireland eagerly foretold in bardic song has in the event given rise to a state in which the elected representatives of the people are subservient to an irresponsible ecclesiastical hierarchy. The welfare state in Britain has become hag-ridden with regulations, and full employment has resulted in absenteeism, wasteful personal spending and a lowering of the standard of work. A 'free society' is a beautiful ideal but it is quite impossible of attainment, human nature being what it is.

'Human nature being what it is' would appear therefore to be the stumbling-block in any move forward to genuine freedom. It is because this consideration has been left out of account by builders of the New Jerusalem that the foundations have given way. The liberalism of the nineteenth century was 'moonstruck with optimism'—to use William James's notable phrase in another context. John Stuart Mill really did believe that men were the best judges of their own self-interest, and he and others looked forward to that 'stationary state' in which there would be the perfect balance of supply and demand, wages and profits, rent and interest, freedom and authority. Tennyson visualized a parliament of man and a federation of the world, and Maurice, Kingsley and the Christian Socialists made a small beginning with self-governing workshops whose very existence depended on a factor which was discovered to be missing, namely a genuine altruism. All utopias have come to grief on the rock of original sin, and our generation, while it is willing and even eager to admit the failure, is strenuously unwilling to admit the cause of it. Consequently men put their trust in ideology, in machinery, in pacts and concordats and treaties, every one of which assumes that men will abide by their promises. The Psalmist praised the righteous man who 'sweareth unto his neighbour, and disappointeth him not: though it were to his own hindrance', but this kind of righteousness in these days is in very short supply.

Granted then that human sin is the real root of all our troubles, is there any way of so ordering society that the devices and designs of sinful men may be neutralized, or, alternatively, that men's instincts for peace and good will shall be made regulative over all the rest?

## 2 THE 'GOOD NEIGHBOUR'

In such an inquiry we must be on our guard against two assumptions. The first I have already indicated—it is the assumption that a moral society can exist apart from moral men. The second is the assumption that moral men will of themselves constitute a moral society. It has often been assumed by Christian people that if only all men were Christians the resulting society could take care of itself. This over-simplification of the issue has been one cause of so much ineffectiveness in Christian thinking on social and political questions. The relations of people to one another in society raise issues which are present whether men are Christians or not.

Let us take two illustrations.

What ought to be the policy of the Australian Government towards immigration from Japan? The easy 'Christian' answer is 'Let them all come', and if the world were governed by love and good will it would appear that this was the only proper answer. On the other hand, to allow unlimited immigration of people with a much lower standard of living into a continent which has a high standard of living not only lowers the general standard all round but also puts thousands of people out of work. To rob Peter to pay Paul is not only false economics but it can scarcely be called Christian. If all Japanese and all Australians were God-fearing church members the problem would still be there. And this problem is not peculiar to this situation alone. Lord Keynes pointed out that full employment, if it is to be world-wide, will inevitably mean the acceptance by many people of a lower standard of living than that which they now enjoy. How can this problem be solved by simple personal acceptance of the Christian faith?

Again, what is the proper Christian procedure in a mixed society where, say, a majority of people are Christians and the others are not? Should we wait for unanimity? Is it the Christian thing for a majority to coerce the minority? Or is it wise, out of true gentlemanly and Christian feeling, for the minority to be allowed to frustrate the will of the majority? In the United States some years ago we saw the working of one of these kinds of coercion. Prohibition of alcoholic liquor was hailed by many of the churches as a glorious triumph of Christian principles. The consequences, however, were so appalling and led to such a lowering of moral standards that the prohibition had to be repealed.

All such beliefs as these rest on a rooted conviction that companies of men can be brought to act in the same way as individual men, and that the ethics of the 'good neighbour' are the same for the group as for the individual. Consequently in some theological quarters there has been a harking back to the days of Aquinas or of Calvin, when this identification was accepted, in the hope that we may find in these ancient writers the guidance that we need in our present discontents. But their times are not our times nor their ways our ways. The pattern of society that they had in mind was that of the village community where every man knew his neighbour, where buying and selling went on before the eyes of all, where supply and demand could roughly be foreseen and adjusted, and where the community was at hand to deal with disagreements. Even where the village community had given way to the town the thinking about this question still presupposed its continued existence. But in these days when our breakfast coffee comes from Brazil, our cereals from North America, our bacon from Denmark, our sugar from the West Indies, how can we possibly assemble the simple equation which will enable us to pay our neighbour the 'just price'? The neighbour nowadays may well be someone we have never seen, someone of a different nationality, of a different race and colour and creed, living at the ends of the earth. The relations between us may be governed by factors for which none of us is responsible and which indeed few of us understand. The belief that all political and social problems are at bottom moral problems is a dangerous popular simplification. Being half a truth it is also half a lie, and it does not help us much in our present situation. Ours is a world mechanized, industrialized, urbanized and international. Both its oneness and its separateness are features of an entirely different kind from any that have been seen in the past.

There is a further consideration to be kept in mind in view of the upsurge of nationalism in Africa and the East. The political development of these nations has hitherto been dependent on the West, and Western culture has been for nearly two thousand years impregnated with Christian principles even though it may have turned aside from Christian practice. But today over a large part of the earth's surface there is an indignant rejection of the Christian way of life. This is true of practically the whole of the continent of Asia, including Asiatic Russia, China, India and Burma. Mr Nehru, with singular ignorance of history, has referred to Christianity as a Western religion, and the new national states of the East have come to look upon Christianity as both alien and hostile. The African situation was until recently somewhat different, for animism has no sacred books such as are found in Hinduism or Buddhism to act as a substitute for the Christian Bible. The tremendous growth of Islam, however, in West Africa, has given many Africans an alternative which they feel to be more consistent than the Gospel, while many of those who have grown up under Christian mission influences have become increasingly uneasy at the connexion between European suzerainty and the Christian Church. Certain questions, therefore, are unavoidable. How is it possible even to think of a Christian sociology when one half of the world is not Christian at all? Whence are to come the spiritual sanctions which alone will make possible an unselfish community life, and how can there be such a thing as a 'free society' when people's views about freedom are so widely diverse? Political thinking in these days must take into account the brutal fact that the old foundations of Western life in Roman law, Greek philosophy and Christian ethics are not shared by the continent of Asia, nor are they accepted at any rate for the time being by the mighty Russian empire. Moreover, the East, not content with a rejection of Christianity, is concerned to replace it with something else. In 1957 the Prime Minister of Ceylon opened in Colombo a training school for Buddhist monks. An appeal was made for one million rupees to enable Buddhist missionaries to be sent to Germany 'to spread the light of the Gospel of Buddhism in darkest Europe'.

## 3 DEFINITIONS

Clearly such a situation as this requires a reorientation of the idea of the Church and the idea of the State.

Of the Church it is needed because ethics are now no longer merely domestic, whereas the Church's concern in the past has been primarily with personal relations on a small and intimate scale. It is needed also because in these bitter forty years of war and its aftermath the Church itself has come under the fire of judgement. It cannot in these days rest upon a 'fugitive and cloistered virtue' which slinks out of the arena in which men are struggling both for their lives and for their integrity. It has been accustomed to judge men and nations. It has now had to recognize that all judgement must begin at the house of God. The priest or the parson, the elder or the deacon, the theologian or the missionary, is a man of like passions with other men, and he is under judgement like other men. Any judgement he makes comes back upon himself and he is at once non-suited in any claim he may make for exemption. Even the impressive façade of the Church of Rome has shown cracks under this strain. The movement started by the worker priests of France was symptomatic of a much greater hunger and thirst after righteousness than the hierarchy could appreciate, let alone supply.

And further, such a reorientation of the idea of the Church is needed because in Protestantism at any rate, the 'impregnable rock of Holy Scripture' as Mr Gladstone called it, and in the sense in which he meant it, has ceased to be an adequate or even an appropriate foundation for the faith. Yet in a quite different historical, rather than dogmatic, sense the Bible has a far more secure and defensible position as the rule of faith and standard of conduct than ever before. But this new knowledge is as yet the property of a small minority, and it not only requires a more widespread acceptance but it also needs to be worked out as a rule by which men live and by which they are prepared to die. This was the strength of the old belief in verbal inspiration and it needs to be recaptured. Meanwhile the old authorities, Roman and revivalist, are having it all their own way, and the curious thing is that so often the modern scientist, keener on certainty than on truth, finds this dogmatic position singularly attractive. To know where one stands, especially in a world of flux like the present, is a most desirable object. It would seem therefore that there needs also to be a reorientation of Protestantism as a whole. There are, however, many inescapable difficulties, some of which we shall consider in the following pages.

The State, too, is changing. We shall notice shortly that progressive states—that is, those states where the Government expect from time to time to lose an election and to have people with other views and policy put in their place—are developing more and more the idea of the State as society instead of simply the government or the official class. The family, consciously, or unconsciously, is becoming a pattern for politics which enlightened statesmen tend to follow and seek to realize. This in itself brings a new crop of difficulties. Concern for the several members of the family may be and indeed is exploited, and the beneficiaries of the Welfare State become so fascinated by their new rights as to lose sight of their old obligations. The elementary fact that benefits must be paid for and can be paid for only out of taxation takes on the appearance of a compulsory levy by an alien authority for no obvious purpose. The time gap between payment and benefit may be so wide that one side is not discernible from the other, and the very people who benefit will be most uncooperative when the time for payment comes round. Furthermore, the inclusion of all citizens within the family of the State has brought about a shift of power from politics to industry. Organized labour and even labour that is not organized have a power in the community which can out-manœuvre any merely political device used against them. It is impossible to send to gaol an entire trade union, and where large masses of men are concerned it makes no difference at all whether their actions are declared to be illegal or not. The futility of such an attempt was seen in 1926 when Sir John Simon in three speeches proved that the strike was illegal. The only fit question to ask about such a declaration was 'So what?'—a question to which there was no answer.

It is obvious, therefore, that the idea of the State as well as that of the Church needs overhauling. And such overhauling needs to be practical. The world is sick of ideologies, as they are called, whether they are translated into practice as in Soviet Russia, or whether they exhibit only the cleverness of the disgruntled intellectual or the crude longing for power of the half-educated.

The relations of Church and State can be considered either in terms of the secular world in which we all find ourselves or in the general terms of the ideal free society which we hope to create and in which we hope to live. If we have in mind the present secular world we shall think of Church and State as institutions. From this point of view (and this alone) the Church is no more than a trade union or any other voluntary society. Indeed so closely akin is the Church to a trade union that many of those who profess to stand for what is called the 'Catholic' position are the very people who insist on the Church's being a 'closed shop'. A 'high' doctrine of the Church tends to result in an attempt to glorify the institution *as such*. (There are no 'high' or 'low' Roman Catholics; the terms are in use simply within Protestantism.) But an institution is not a divine society, whether Roman, Anglican or Free Church, simply because its members *say* that it is. And it is not always easy to see the marks of divinity in a body which has buildings and caretakers, pays taxes and insurance, and runs a magazine. The relation of such a body to the State is that of an organized unofficial society to the Great Society, the official State. In Catholic countries these relations are often the subject of concordats. These are of the nature of written constitutions by which the relations of Church and State are given a contractual basis. Such for instance was the concordat that Mussolini made with the Pope, and the even more interesting one signed on 27 August 1953 between the Vatican and the Spanish Government.[1] The contracting parties meet as equals, the one ecclesiastical and the other political. A concordat is a record not so much of their concord as of their differences, and at bottom it represents an arrangement between two diverse groups of men scrambling for power. The community at large is not a party to the proceedings and the worldly good of the institution is the only matter of concern. This type of relationship has characterized Byzantine Christianity from the very beginning. It resulted in politics being reserved wholly to the State but sanctioned by the Church, while 'spiritual' matters were reserved wholly to the Church protected by the State. This hand-in-glove policy made the Church completely ineffective as a challenge to the State, while religion degenerated into ritual and little else. No Western country, not even Italy, witnessed to such spiritual ineffectiveness as was shown by the Church in Russia under the Czars.

One matter which stands in the way of a free world is national and sectional sovereignty. It is quite impossible for unity to be achieved among the nations or among the churches unless each unit is willing to forswear its own sovereignty, and this is an attitude that cannot be adopted by calculations of profit and loss. Church and nation alike are peopled by ordinary human beings who are naturally jealous guardians of what they conceive to be their 'heritage'. It is of no account whether this heritage is conceived in ecclesiastical or in political or in social terms. It is guarded by the same human nature in every case. This idea of the heritage has in it if properly used, after the manner of the man in the parable who had five talents, a source of strength and an inspiration to progress. But unfortunately there is nothing so flattering to sinful human nature than this conception of guardianship of something precious that has come down to us from the

[1] See below, pp. 106ff.

past. It is used to stall all efforts of change or development and, so used or rather misused, is a rationalization of pride and selfishness. We shall return to this subject again, but meanwhile it is to be noted that the Church is in a very weak position in appealing to the nations for the greater good of the world to lay aside their sovereignty and cease to be judges in their own case when the denominations themselves have no intention of giving up their own sovereignty for the greater good of the Kingdom of God.

The very conception of a 'free society' emphasizes that we are all living in the one world, created, as we believe, by God to be a home for mankind. How competent is either the Church or the State at home-making? The Church has the greater claim because, in spite of all its defects, it does stand for spiritual values and it does seek to bring men into communion with God whose Fatherhood is the pledge of human brotherhood. It has the opportunity to affirm the spiritual basis of human life, and to offer men that sense of security of which the symbol is not an impregnable fortress but a loving family. The only genuine security that persons can ever have lies in the good will of other persons. The relations of Church and State therefore must be determined by the free society in which we all wish to live. It cannot be determined by an adjustment of claims. The Catholic assertion that the Church and the State are both 'perfect societies' means precisely nothing in a world of three hundred or more Christian denominations, where the Church has for the most part lost control over social welfare, literature, science, art, commerce and education. In regard to these matters we rightly refer to the present regimes, for instance, in Spain and Southern Ireland, as 'survivals', and survivals are an unconscionable time a-dying. Yet as the State is becoming more and more coincident with the community, the Church is showing more and more marks of its characteristic original pattern of a lay society. The Church will never redeem the world so long as it continues to be a hierarchical caste. It may conquer the world as it did in the days of Constantine, but Dante's lament that the sword had been joined to the crook indicates that conquest is quite a different thing from redemption.

CHAPTER II

# THE CHURCH IN THE WORLD (1)

## 1 VARIOUS MEANINGS OF 'CHURCH'

Sir George Cornwall Lewis in 1832 wrote a very interesting book, *On the Use and Abuse of some Political Terms*. It was a sort of commentary on Dr Johnson's maxim 'Clear your mind of cant'. There is need for something to be written on the use and abuse of some ecclesiastical terms, where cant is perhaps even more evident. Both political and ecclesiastical terms often have the effect of deceiving both the people who hear them used and those who use them. And of all these terms the word 'Church' needs most clarification.

The 'Church' can mean a body of Christian people meeting for worship and mutual edification, or a particular denomination of Christians, or the sum total of all the Christian denominations, or a supernatural society founded in visible form by Christ, or an invisible supernatural society cutting across all denominations, or an organized institution owning property and investments. Here are six definitions and they can be further extended according to the form of Church government which we emphasize. It may be essentially a hierarchy in which the laymen take no responsible part but simply carry out orders, it may be essentially a lay body with certain full-time officers duly appointed by the people, or it may be a society of friends with no distinction at all between lay and clerical. And again we may draw distinctions between churches in which the priesthood is believed to possess certain supernatural powers, those in which the preaching of the word and administration of the sacraments are for edification and are not associated with specific authority, and those which have neither sacraments nor separated ministry nor official creed.

Here indeed is room for vast confusion, and as if this were not enough there is further complication introduced by the loose use of the word 'catholic'. The Methodist Church for instance is said to 'cherish its place in the Holy Catholic Church',[1] a statement which completely puzzles the outsider and is more of a protestation than a description. Anglo-Catholics resent the appropriation of the word 'catholic' by the Romanists and yet their own definition is repudiated by Roman Catholics and by every other brand of Protestantism. The Roman Catholic position is quite simple, for by the 'Holy Catholic Church' they mean themselves, with or without the schismatic Greek Orthodox. They do not consider Anglicans, nor even Anglo-Catholics, as having any title to the adjective at all, while the use of the term by Methodists and other late arrivals on the ecclesiastical scene seems extremely absurd. Unfortunately all these protestations seem to indicate that the term 'catholic' has come to have what is called in other circles a 'snob value' and is freely used without any pretence of exactitude except as a quick way of 'unchurching' those with whom one does not happen to agree. Meanwhile when the man in the street has occasion to mention the 'Catholics' he means Roman Catholics and nobody else.[2]

## 2 THE IDEAL AS A SANCTION FOR THE INSTITUTION

There are, however, two main uses of the word 'Church' which are helpful in our present inquiry and which have to be kept separate. The first is the Church as a corporate institution, inhabiting buildings, owning property, publishing newspapers, having its own officers, and containing all sorts of people not always distinguishable from those who are outside. This also includes recognition of the fact that the 'Church' in this regard is not one institution but many denominations. The other sense of the word is more difficult to define. It is an ideal society, the general body of Christians of many denominations and of none, a cross-section of all the churches and, as St Augustine believed, probably leaving out quite a number of people included in the

[1] The Deed of Union, 1932.
[2] See Appendix, below, p. 182.

first lot and including some that are there excluded. When we discuss 'the Church and war' or 'the Church and gambling' we are using the word 'Church' in this general sense. It is not quite the same as what is often called the 'Church invisible' in which people usually include those Christians who have passed through the gates of death, but in so far as it is represented by no specific organization it too can be called 'invisible'. If we could give the old word 'Christendom' a spiritual rather than a political meaning that is just about the sense in which we could here use the word 'Church'. In argument it is sometimes referred to simply as 'Christianity' or the 'Gospel', set in contrast against the organized churches.

The importance of keeping these two meanings quite separate lies in the twofold relationship between them. Each can be related to the other positively as a sanction and a justification, or it can be related negatively as an ideal and a challenge. An institution may seek to justify itself in the name of the larger Christianity, while by other people, also in the name of the larger Christianity, it may be criticized and even condemned. These two relationships—sanction and challenge—we shall find in another context when we come to a discussion of the State, for the State too has its ideal as well as its material form.

Where the invisible Church is used as a sanction for the institution and identified with it the institution thus becomes a law unto itself, owning no higher authority. No doubt in the last resort it will agree that it is subordinate to the invisible Church whose head is Christ, but as it is left to itself to determine what is and what is not the mind of Christ the reasoning would appear to be circular. In the later Middle Ages in Europe the Conciliar movement came up against a similar difficulty. It was agreed on all hands that a General Council was above the Pope, but as only the Pope could summon a General Council not much was gained by the agreement. It is parallel to the situation where the directors of a company are ultimately controlled by the shareholders' meeting, but it is the directors who decide what shall come before the shareholders' meeting. The New Testament may be said to be of higher authority than the Church, but as the Church is held to be the sole interpreter of the New Testament we do not get very much further.

This, however, is not a specifically Roman Catholic attitude. It is found in other churches also. A recent example comes from South Africa. The newspaper report is as follows:

*Johannesburg*, 8 April 1957

The Council of the Dutch Reformed Church of South Africa stated to-day that no violence would be done to the Church's principles by a clause in the Native Laws Amendment Bill empowering the Minister of Native Affairs, Dr Verwoerd, to debar people from corporate worship on the grounds of colour.

Consequently it remained satisfied with the bill, it was added. The statement read:

'Consultation took place with the Minister with reference to the following principles:

'1. The Gospel of Jesus Christ emanates from God to all mankind and is subject to no human limitations;

'2. The task is laid on the Church of Christ to proclaim the Gospel throughout the world and to all peoples;

'3. The right to determine how, when, and to whom the Gospel shall be proclaimed is exclusively in the competence of the Church.

'4. It is the duty of the State, as a servant of God, to allow freedom to the Church in the execution of its divine calling and to respect the sovereignty of the Church in its own sphere.'[1]

The identification of the physical organization with the spiritual community makes every issue that touches the institution a matter of concern in the heavenly regions. If the Government of a country, for instance, refuses to give it a grant for its schools it is held that it is not the institution alone that suffers but also God Himself. This attitude is a form of spiritual blackmail and makes all discussion extremely difficult.[2]

An even more subtle way of calling in the invisible to redress

[1] *Manchester Guardian*, 9 April 1957. In this statement clause 3 is clearly in opposition to clause 1.

[2] 'It should not appear part of the politics of eternity that Michael's sister's son obtains a particular post beginning at thirty shillings a week'; A.E., *Thoughts for a Convention: Memorandum on the State of Ireland* (1917), p. 13.

the balance of the visible is to be found in the development of doctrines that are characteristic of particular denominations. For example, it is well known that no professional historian of repute has been able to discover documentary evidence to justify the claim that the ministry of certain Christian Churches has descended in an unbroken chain from the apostles themselves. This might be supposed completely to settle the matter, but in actual fact it makes no difference whatever. As Newman said about Noah's ark, 'the preservation of our race in Noah's ark is an historical fact which history would never arrive at without Revelation'.[1] The appeal is not really to history at all but to dogma (by Newman called 'revelation') and is addressed to an invisible court of opinion which is held to be competent to vouch that the facts are as they are desired to be. 'That which always, everywhere, and by everybody has been believed' is accepted as a self-evident truth in these matters just as in the Middle Ages it was held to justify the Ptolemaic theory of the universe.

Newman put the matter plainly in his *Development of Christian Doctrine*, which although published as far back as 1845 is nevertheless highly relevant to some of the controversies of our own time. He accepted the fact that Rome has developed very considerably since apostolic times and he admitted the existence of what Protestants call 'accretions' to the original Gospel. These, however, he asserts, are not all accretions at all, for they are not alien to the Gospel but are the natural outcome of principles inherent within it. Not all developments, however, are to be accepted. The decision as to what are and what are not 'true' developments requires the existence of a continuing infallible authority, and it is upon this authority rather than upon the historical facts of its origin that the Church now rests. The Pope represents an invisible authority which is regulative of the Church itself and even, apparently, of Church history. By identifying this authority with the external fact of the Papacy Newman of course was assuming that which he was really required to prove and he accordingly misapplied the quite sound principle from which he started. He

[1] *Discourses on University Education* (Everyman edition), p. 64.

admitted that he was using a 'hypothesis to account for a difficulty',[1] or in other words a convenient method of side-stepping the inconveniences of history. The recent promulgation of the dogma of the Assumption of the Virgin illustrates this very point, for there admittedly is no historical evidence whatever for such belief. The belief therefore has nothing to do with a historical event but only with an authority presumed to be infallible. It is noteworthy, however, that when that authority promulgates a new dogma it is always assumed that far from being new it has really been there from the beginning although not fully revealed until now.

It is through lack of appreciation of this situation that books such as the late Bishop Barnes's *The Rise of Christianity* or even the many learned works of the late Dr G. G. Coulton fail to carry conviction in their main aim. They attack the Catholic position on historical grounds which are not the grounds on which it is really based.

So far we have considered the use of the invisible Church as a sanction for the visible institution. But the converse process is also at work, for it is the visible which gives shape and content to the invisible. The New Jerusalem may be a city coming down from God out of heaven, but it is nevertheless recognizable as a city, with streets and gates and buildings and people walking about. The ideal can never be wholly ideal because we are limited even in the deepest things of the spirit to categories which we ourselves know. We cannot conceive the unknown except in terms of the known. The very notion of an invisible body providing a sanction for a visible institution implies some measure of identification between the two. It is not surprising, therefore, to find the specifications of the City of God laid down with both clearness and confidence by Aquinas and Calvin and the Fathers of the Church both Catholic and Protestant. Yet the characteristic feature of an invisible Church is its invisibility. To give it a local

[1] J. H. Newman, *An Essay on the Development of Christian Doctrine* (1845), p. 27. See R. A. Knox, *The Belief of Catholics* (1927), p. 233: 'to believe in Catholic doctrines without believing in the existence of that infallible authority which guarantees them all is to hold, not the Catholic faith but a series of speculative opinions.'

habitation and a name may be inevitable in the light of the working of the human mind but it necessarily weakens its force both as a sanction and as a challenge. Even those denominations which would hold to the essential invisibility of the Church as contrasted with its visible manifestation in the individual congregation could scarcely avoid endowing the invisible Church with qualities that perhaps belong elsewhere.

The relations of Church and State are accordingly affected by these various relationships within the Church itself. The institution as such is related to the State in the same way as any other society, trade union, industrial concern, club or association. The only difference is where one particular church is 'established'. The Church as an ideal, however, if used as a sanction for the institution, brings into the relations of Church and State a metaphysical and an emotional element which are not present in the case of a trade union or a club. Yet if the invisible Church is to be a challenge to the institution it can scarcely avoid being a challenge to *all* institutions, including the State itself. It is to this second aspect of the invisible Church as a challenge rather than a sanction that we must now turn.

CHAPTER III

# THE CHURCH IN THE WORLD (2)

## I THE IDEAL AS A CHALLENGE TO THE INSTITUTION

Christianity, or Christendom, in the sense in which I have used the terms, the general body of Christians, the invisible Church, 'Christianity' or the 'Gospel'—using all these, for the sake of convenience, as equivalents—can be not only a sanction for the institution but also and more often a challenge to it. This invisible community knows no barriers of race, nation, colour or class, whereas the institution all too often exhibits such distinctions.

The existence of this community is a fundamental necessity in the thought of those who would seek to reform the visible institution. Reformers are always three-parts traditionalists. They appeal over the head of the existing institution to some ideal in the past or in the future, some unwritten charter in the mind of man. They are concerned not so much with the rejection of one authority as with the search for another. Anarchy, or the rejection of *all* authority, is a pathological condition and in the history of religion makes very rare appearances. Yet the mere recognition of an ideal, apart altogether from individual reformers, known or unknown, who make their appeal to it, is a standing challenge to the institution. There is such a thing as the silent influence of a perpetually uplifted standard even if it has no external means of enforcing its acceptance. Some reforms come about almost by the mere attrition that is inherent in an evil system.

The stock example, of course, is slavery, which was accepted by the ancient world (including the Church) and, in places, by the Christian world right down to the nineteenth century as an inevitable factor in a stable social structure. The ideal Christian community, however, the Church invisible, the Kingdom of God, by whatever name it is called, is a society in which there is neither Jew nor Greek, barbarian nor Scythian, male nor female, bond nor free, but all are 'one in Christ Jesus'. In due course the continual pressure of this ideal has been too much for the institution itself and it has had to change. The Christian community came gradually but with conviction to condemn slavery as contrary to the Gospel.

And along with slavery as an institution go all other forms of exploitation of human beings. It is therefore with a real shock that we read of the Dutch Reformed Church of South Africa appealing to Scripture to justify the permanent helotry of the African race.

Some years ago I was travelling in Nyasaland with a delightful young minister of that Church who was a missionary in those parts. He had a degree of a famous American university and he had a modern outlook on the Bible and the Church. We got on so well that finally I ventured to ask him to explain to me the *religious* grounds of 'apartheid'. In his answer he went back on all that he himself had appeared to believe concerning the historical use of the Bible. He said it was simply this: 'Genesis ix. 25 says "Cursed be Canaan; a servant of servants shall he be unto his brethren".' And Canaan was by him quite gratuitously identified with the South African Bantu. Here was a verse violently wrenched from its context and given an interpretation which has nothing whatever to do with it. Against all this sort of thing the Gospel offers a standing reproach and challenge.

And in these days we have come to see the solvent effect of the Gospel upon any attempt to justify on Christian grounds war or unrestricted capitalism. War may be inevitable in certain situations, but if so it comes as a judgement upon those who have the affairs of the nations in their hands and have not properly exercised their stewardship.

Here, however, we are treading upon the ground of relations between Church and State which will occupy us more fully later. Our concern at the moment is with the invisible Church as a challenge to the Church itself rather than to the State.

## 2 THE CROSS IN HUMAN LIFE

At the centre of the Christian faith is the Cross of Christ. This has become for us such a commonplace symbol that it is often totally forgotten that it was an event before it was a symbol. Somewhere round the year A.D. 29 Jesus of Nazareth was visited with the most shameful and shocking death that could befall any man, Jew or Roman. He shared the fate of the lowest type of criminal as well as of the victims of persecution. Yet by doing so he redeemed the people with whom he was associated, not only the victims of cruelty but even the agents of that cruelty. These like himself were all partakers in our human nature. It was the evil in their nature that crucified him and it was the goodness in his that redeemed them. The view that human nature has to be assessed by the lowest common denominator, something which we share with the beasts, is here shown to be only half the truth. Our human nature undoubtedly has its animal side which, if indulged, can sink a man to the lowest hell, but it has also its divine side which can respond to the promptings of the spirit of God. A questionnaire addressed to the whole human race would never reveal its true inwardness so much as a contemplation of this one solitary event, the crucifixion of Christ. Both the baseness in man and the divinity in man came together at this point.

O Love of God, O sin of man,
In this dread act your strength is tried,
And victory remains with love,
Jesus, my Lord, is crucified.

It is not surprising that the shocking instrument of this execution—the rough cross of wood—should have become a symbol of the forces of good and evil, of love and hate that are at work in the world of human affairs wherein are also worked out the purposes of God for mankind. And although there are other faiths in the world which have other views of God and other views of the nature of the world, it has nevertheless been true that this ambivalence (to use a Freudian term) in all human life has been more effectively exhibited in the event of which the Cross is the symbol than in any other way. Buddhism, Islam, Hinduism—to take three of the great world religions—have each certain elements which are also to be found in a measure in Christianity, but none of them has a cross, and so, while each has its contemplative side and can certainly point the way to individual salvation, none of them has in it that social quality of 'the redemption of the world' which in the Christian faith is, and is alone, 'through our Lord Jesus Christ'. The only truly comparative method of the study of religions is to be found not in comparing them one with another but rather in comparing the ways in which they respectively deal with the stern facts of the human situation as we know it. It is not what they say about themselves that matters but what they have to say about sin, greed, lust, pride, cruelty on the one hand, and, on the other, about redemption from all this. The 'works of the flesh' as well as 'the fruits of the Spirit' are equally factors in the scheme of man's salvation.

Here then we are at the heart of things. The Cross is the standard that is lifted up by which all the associations of mankind in Church and State are to be judged. But what has happened in history? 'In this sign conquer' was the legend in the sky seen by Constantine at the battle of the Milvian Bridge, but it was misread by him as it has constantly been misread all down the ages. What is it that has to be conquered? To Constantine it was the forces of Maxentius, to Charlemagne it was the Saxons, to the barbarian fanatics of the first Crusade it was the cultured Saracens. It was the emblem of the Papal armies in the wars of the Italian republics and has been used in battle right down to our times. This symbol, which has nothing to do with Roman or Greek, Italian or Gaul, Protestant or Catholic, but only with the central riddle of our common humanity, has been taken up as the private possession of a section, cheapened and desecrated and blasphemed in so doing. Here the institution has not only identified the invisible society with itself but has also taken over this universal symbol as a party favour. And the central figure of Calvary has been reproduced in miniature in wood and ivory and silver and gold to be worn on the watch-chain or at the girdle, and has been endowed with magical virtues to which the great original himself laid no claim. The 'challenge of the Cross', however, remains, and nowhere is it a greater challenge than to those who would, as it were, make use of it to enforce their own copyright in things divine.

The Cross represents the real challenge of Christianity to the world and also to the Church. What it means in political terms we shall consider later. But in religious terms it involves a continual charge laid upon Christian people to follow in the footsteps of the Master. If his was the way of the Cross, and if along that road alone came the saving of men from sin and frustration, those who serve him are committed to that way of life if they would carry forward the perpetual work of man's redemption. There are, however, two ways in which the Cross has been misused, and they both arise from that primary drive of the human spirit to obtain control of every situation in which it finds itself. This is the very negation of the religious attitude and cannot be equated with it. But this has not kept men from unconsciously making the attempt. One way of doing this is to claim a knowledge and a power in divine things which are not given to ordinary men. This is the danger in every closed ecclesiastical or theological system and it is the danger inherent in Fundamentalism as well as in Catholicism or modernism. God, instead of being, in the words of von Hügel, a 'vast surplusage', the High and Holy One, becomes limited to our own understanding of Him, even when we are affirming in words his greatness and his 'otherness'. Another way for more ordinary folk is by the reduction of Deity to the level of our ordinary humanity. For instance, to many people the phrase 'the mother of God' is utterly shocking and blasphemous. It is bad enough on the lips of Catholic piety, but it is even worse when it comes in a book such as D. L. Munby's *Christianity and Economic Problems* (1956). It is a phrase which panders to this primary desire which I have just mentioned, for at bottom it is a way of maintaining one's self-respect in the presence of Deity. I have a mother, and so God is like me, for he also has a mother! What crude anthropomorphism is this, masquerading as reverence? Yet there is an unholy kind of holiness which does not shrink from, so to speak, patronizing God himself. It shows itself in the contemplation of the helpless babe in swaddling clothes lying in a manger—

> Little Jesus, wast Thou shy
> Once and just so small as I?—

and also in morbidly dwelling on the physical sufferings of Christ. Men have been found to survey the wondrous cross and to do nothing else but survey it. It has purged them of the passion of pity without in the very least impelling them to go themselves along the same road. This is the real danger which has to be faced and overcome in every sacramental type of religion. Experience is apt to become a closed circle beginning and ending with itself.

We are to be concerned in this book with the relations of Church and State in a free society. Their relations can be sound only if they are both able to accept the same standards of human excellence. If, however, 'the Church' has a merely inbred life of its own, incapable of reaching out to the problems and needs of men and women, we are left simply with an institution that has to be fitted into the social pattern just like any trade union or voluntary society. These considerations therefore, which may appear to be purely theological and even theoretical, are of the first importance, for they provide or fail to provide that incentive which would enable the Church to be the conscience of the community.

## 3 CATHOLICISM AND PROTESTANTISM

I have spoken of the invisible Church as a challenge to the earthly institution. We now come within sight of the distinction that has here to be drawn between Catholicism and Protestantism. We have seen that it is of the essence of Catholicism that it identifies the existing denomination with the invisible Church or the Kingdom of God, and that the institution thus becomes a law unto itself and is in all matters a judge in its own cause. We have also seen the enormous strength that comes to the institution from such identification. But while this attitude has again and again also been that of Protestantism and is indeed characteristic of what Hensley Henson called the 'Protestant underworld', it is nevertheless of the essence of Protestantism that it should not be so. The institution stands all the while under judgement of the Church as a whole and is not a law unto itself.

Protestantism has undergone many changes since the Council of Speyer, and modern Protestantism is not to be explained in terms of either Luther or Calvin. To attempt to do so is to instal those reformers into the position left vacant by Thomas Aquinas and to credit them with a special degree of inspiration not vouchsafed to their successors. It is also completely alien to the spirit of Protestantism. Furthermore, the Protestant attitude to history is by no means the same as the Catholic and to speak of the 'Protestant tradition' may easily be a misuse of terms. Strictly speaking, there cannot be a Protestant tradition except by a denial of the essence of Protestantism. The genuine tradition of Christian experience must be the same for all denominations. In addition no doubt Catholicism has a special tradition of its own which it puts on the same level as the Christian tradition. But the Protestant tradition is to have no tradition which is separate from that of Christianity itself. It was once held that Protestantism stands or falls by the use of the Bible as the inerrant Word of God and the rule of faith and conduct. Consequently when the movement of 'higher criticism' arrived in Europe and America it was felt that the very foundations of the faith were shaken. But it has proved not to be so. Protestantism, like Christianity itself, rests on a far surer base than the verbal inspiration of the Bible. Not being a law unto itself it can welcome truth from whatever quarter it may come. If it rejects verbal inspiration and accepts a historical interpretation of the Bible so also it rejects the verbal inspiration of the creeds. Its attitude to history is that of a community which itself exists within the process in which history is continually being made. The note of authenticity is not that of dogma or organization but of the continued reappearance of the life of Christ in the souls of men. This of course applies to Catholicism also, for Protestantism has no monopoly of personal religion, but in Catholicism this is not regulative as it essentially is in Protestantism.

It is interesting to notice in this respect the standard of orthodoxy of that most truly Protestant denomination, the Society of Friends. It is commonly said that the Friends or Quakers have no creed. In a sense that is true, but only in the sense that no assent to a statement of doctrine is required in order to join the Society. But in the first of the three volumes of the Quaker 'Book of Discipline' sixty pages are given to accounts of the 'spiritual experiences of Friends'. There are in all thirty-four short testimonies from every rank of society—scholars, bankers, housewives, landed gentry, blacksmiths, politicians and servant girls. There is a large variety not only of background and education but also of temperament, but the central experiences are recognizably similar. 'Orthodoxy' in the Quaker sense would appear to be conformity to this type of Christian life, and this has been found definite enough and strong enough to sustain the Society's witness over three centuries. Baron von Hügel, the eminent Roman Catholic theologian, used to maintain that the Quakers were a true church, although, he added, 'a church in miniature'.

It is of the genius of Christianity and particularly of Protestantism that it has a progressive attitude to truth. This, in theological language, follows from its belief in the Holy Spirit leading men into more and more truth as they are obedient to the light that they already have. An institution, however, cannot but have 'articles of association'. It has to define itself somehow, and therefore in the very nature of things there has to be in every organized church, even the Society of Friends, a certain measure of rigidity which is in apparent contrast to the concept of the Church universal. It is a difficult question to know just where to draw the line beyond which in one direction rigidity becomes betrayal and in the other direction freedom becomes licence. The drawing of this line is of importance in the relations of Church and State, for it marks the distinction between the Church as an organization and the Church as a spirit.

Protestantism, however, like democracy (as we shall see later), has the weakness of its most characteristic virtue. Believing, as it does, in guidance by the Spirit, and recognizing that it is itself under judgement, and refusing to be judge in its own cause, it is ill fitted for action in a crisis whether within the walls of the specific institution or in relation to the world outside. Suspense of judgement is far more characteristic of Protestantism than even justification by faith or the priesthood of all believers or any other of the weapons from the armoury of the sixteenth century. This is due to a certain inevitable agnosticism about the possible rightness or wrongness of its action and a rejection of the very idea of infallibility. It is not so in the Roman Church. The Church knows exactly where it stands on every issue and need look to no endorsement from outside. It has a catena of rules of casuistry ready to be applied in any emergency. This gives it a certain 'political' advantage, although I believe that in the long run this mechanical assurance in matters of the spirit may prove to be its undoing.

A good illustration of the difference between the Catholic and the Protestant attitude will be found in the circumstances of the General Strike in Britain in 1926. Cardinal Bourne at once proclaimed the strike to be a mortal sin, 'a sin against the obedience which we owe to God...and against the charity and brotherly love which are due to our brethren'.[1] He was warmly commended by the Government. Archbishop Davidson of Canterbury, however, felt that there was a good deal to be said on the other side and that if the Government simply broke the strike by force it would leave behind it a legacy of untold bitterness. He therefore urged the Government to have the issue thrashed out in discussion—a counsel, of course, which the Government did not think very helpful. We shall have occasion to return to this illustration again, but it is relevant here as illustrating the strength and the weakness both of the Catholic and of the Protestant mind. At bottom the difference is due to the conception of truth as a dynamic principle rather than as an external fact insulated from circumstances. Clearly, according to one's conception of truth so

[1] G. K. A. Bell, *Randall Davidson*, I, p. 1312. See also the Catholic writer, W. Teeling, *The Pope in Politics* (1937), p. 162.

will be one's view of the relations of Church and State and so also will be one's conception of a 'free society'.

It is not surprising therefore that Protestantism has been more immediately affected by changes in social structure, intellectual climate and political development than the Roman and the Orthodox Churches. The vast improvements in the standard of living in England and America have been due to the spirit of Protestantism, for the contentment with poverty and even squalor which is not unusual in Catholic countries seems to the Protestant mind almost sinful. But as material conditions have become better the minds of men have turned away from religion as no longer a necessary incentive to self-improvement, and it has either become a popular fashion or it has faded away into indifference. The kind of easy Rotarian ethics put out to well-to-do business men in New York by Norman Vincent Peale and in Chicago by Preston Bradley has nothing whatever to do with Christianity as it is properly understood, but it illustrates a danger that awaits a Protestantism that has become too successful. To the average Catholic neither 'staying put' nor 'getting on' seems to be a matter of any particular concern to his church. The growth of urban populations has also affected Protestantism, for city life is a great solvent of religious values of the Protestant type.[1]

The last fifty years have seen incredible changes in the intellectual outlook of the progressive countries of the world. They have not all been due to modern science, although these are the more obvious. The old Prometheus myth has come true, and men have scaled the heavens and brought back the secrets of the universe. Man has become the measure of all things more surely than at the time of the Renaissance, although in these days he has delegated much of his capacity to ingenious machines of his own devising. But in the realm of thought there have been changes which have vitally affected Protestantism. The new cosmology, the comparative study of religion, the development of psychological research, the historical attitude to the Bible, field-work in

[1] A. I. Abell, *The Urban Impact on American Protestantism 1865–1900* (Harvard, 1943).

cultural anthropology and the emergence of sociology as a science have combined to destroy the entire *Weltanschauung* of the earlier Protestantism. To go back behind all this to the ideas of the Reformation period is an academic antiquarianism with no real relevance to the times in which we live.

Political movements at home and abroad have also had considerable influence on Protestantism. The close association of the British Free Churches with the Liberal party has meant that as Liberalism itself has declined, so there has been a corresponding decline of Nonconformity, especially in churches of the Congregationalist type. The Free Churches, which in the nineteenth century were very much the churches of the working classes, were not sufficiently aware of the working class change-over from Liberalism to Labour, and Labour became alienated from the Churches. Abroad, the growth of self-conscious nationalism in Africa and the Far East and the resuscitation of the old ethnic religions has almost re-created for the Church in India and elsewhere the conditions of the Roman Empire of the first century. Christianity, so closely identified with the white ruling classes, has suffered with them in their eclipse. These movements have brought to light certain unexpected differences in the missionary methods of Roman Catholics and Protestants. The Edinburgh Missionary Conference of 1910 brought together almost all the Protestant missionary societies and resulted in the setting-up of the International Missionary Council and the founding of the *International Review of Missions*. It also delimited spheres of missionary activity so that henceforth there should be no overlapping among the Protestant missions. Moreover there was a new respect for the old religions. The word 'heathen' disappeared from missionary literature and it was recognized that God had spoken to all men in some measure in their own religion and that Christianity came not so much to destroy as to fulfil. All this was solid gain. The new spirit in missions, however, went further. It was commonly said—by Dr John R. Mott and others—that we should not know the fullness of Christ until India, Japan, Africa and China had added their characteristic national contributions to the witness of the world to Christ. This was an acknowledgement of nationalism within the universal Gospel which almost amounted to recognizing, say, Indian Christianity as something essentially different from British, American or Chinese Christianity. So much was this the case that about thirty years ago there arose a school of Indian Christian writers who attempted to interpret Christianity in Indian theological terms. A characteristic product of this school of thought was *Jesus the Avatar*, a book by V. Chakkarai, the very title of which was a witness to the Indian depreciation of history. Jesus of Nazareth was not an avatar but a genuine historical person. This movement, however, was bound to right itself in time (as it has done through the new Church of South India), but here and there the new missionary attitude went further and emphasized the national approach as almost regulative of the presentation of the Gospel itself. A new nervousness arose, a new sensitiveness to native opinion, which was no doubt fit and proper so long as it was not treated as of primary concern. To some people, for instance, it seemed more important to save a Chinese from 'loss of face' than to save him from sin. The missionary societies began to be unsure of their message and there were extremists at both ends of the scale—those who went 'native' (a very prominent Y.M.C.A. secretary, for instance, more or less identified Christianity with Buddhism and was believed by some to have died a Buddhist), and those who deplored the whole movement. It was sometimes said of one great missionary society that it had lost all conviction. A book came out at this time with the significant title *Missionary Methods: St Paul's or Ours?*, by Roland Allen, which drew the distinction between what was believed to be the apostolic message to men as men without reference to nationality or race, and the present attitude which put these things first, or at any rate appeared to do so.

The Roman Catholic missionaries' attitude might appear on the surface to be the same. They made use of native dress and customs and, up to a point, of native religion, and indeed they went further than Protestants in giving a measure of autonomy to indigenous churches. At a mission in the Congo the figures on the crucifixes were those of a black Christ. Catholicism in the Congo and Uganda and Japan seemed to have developed as many characteristic racial features as in Spain and England and America. But these never became regulative. The thing that mattered first and last was the central Catholic doctrines and loyalties, which were universal and not local.

Protestantism in Africa and the East recovered itself, but in its deference to the local situation, its unwillingness to dominate and its occasional doubt whether it had any right to be there at all it showed the defects of its qualities. Much the most important feature of the Church of South India is the way in which it has succeeded in presenting the challenge of the universal Gospel within a framework of Indian life and action. It is the New Testament and not the Bhagavadgita that speaks to the soul of India just as it speaks to the soul of England or America or China. At the same time it is the gospel that is universal and not the external organization of the Church. This relation to Indian life and need is far more significant than the fact, so important to Western eyes, that Anglicans, Congregationalists, Presbyterians and Methodists have sunk their denominational differences. It is in South India that the strength of Protestantism is seen without its weakness. The fact that the different denominations have come together in India while they are still apart in the West emphasizes the reliance that the new Church must place upon the invisible Church as regulative of the actions of the institution. It is not a law unto itself, it is not judge in its own cause, but it is nevertheless free to experiment and to adventure and to be guided into new truth.

What Dean Inge has called the 'fissiparous' nature of Protestantism has been held against it as a reproach. It is continually giving rise to fresh divisions, each claiming to be more in accordance with the 'pattern in the mount'[1] than the parent or any other body. When we read of the two hundred and fifty or more Protestant denominations in America and a similar number in

[1] 'See, saith he, that thou make all things according to the pattern shewed to thee in the mount.' Hebrews viii. 5.

South Africa the right of private judgement would appear to have gone mad. However, this is one of the inconveniences that follow from the Protestant position and much of it is due no doubt not to religion at all but to human sinfulness. It very much complicates things for the legislator. In recent years, for instance, the courts of the United States have been greatly exercised by the claim of Jehovah's Witnesses to be a denomination whose full-time ministers, though not ordained, should nevertheless be exempt from military service. Here again, confronted by the massive façade of the Roman Catholic Church, Protestantism appears a thing of bits and pieces. Nevertheless the disunity of Protestantism is apt to be as deceptive as the unity of the Catholic Church. For instance, in the Congo in 1937 there were at work forty-three Protestant missions, a sufficiently alarming evidence of 'fissiparousness'. In the same year, however, there were seventy-nine separate Roman Catholic organizations at work. The Roman missions had, of course, unity of a type quite different from that of the Protestants, who were united only in a voluntary grouping called the Congo Protestant Council. Over against the Government (which was Catholic) the Roman missions could speak with one voice and were therefore in a much stronger strategic position than the Protestants. It is, however, a matter for discussion whether in the long run a strongly centralized type of organization, while most effective for gaining converts to itself, is more effective in christianizing a people than a more loose organization that has to depend more on its own inward life. Early medieval history in the West is a warning against the too easy assumption that conversion may give any more than a veneer of Christianity.

## CHAPTER IV

# STATE AND COMMUNITY

### I VARIOUS MEANINGS OF 'STATE'

We now turn to the 'State' and the various uses that have been made of the word.

In 1776 Tom Paine published his famous pamphlet *Common Sense* in order to stimulate the American colonists to break loose from England. It begins with these words:

> Some writers have so confounded Society with Government, as to leave little or no distinction between them; whereas they are not only different, but have different origins. Society is produced by our wants, and Government by our wickedness; the former promotes our happiness *positively*, by uniting our affections: the latter *negatively*, by restraining our vices. The one encourages intercourse, the other creates distinctions. The first is a patron, the last a punisher.

If we look on the 'State' and the 'Government' as equivalent terms we shall note that Paine trod in the footsteps of Luther to whom the State had its origin in human sin, and that he anticipated Karl Marx, to whom the State was itself sinful, so that when the glorious classless society appeared the State would wither away and die. The factor that distinguishes the State from all other forms of association is the fact that it possesses the physical instruments of coercion. It is this which has brought many Christian people into the same camp with Communists, for no coercion is agreeable and the less we are able to resist it the more we dislike it. The 'State' therefore has been looked upon as something impersonal, inhuman, remote and, from the Christian angle, necessarily 'secular' and atheistic.

The word 'State' has many meanings, but in ordinary speech we mean the Government, acting through its central or local agencies. It is important to realize the local side of government. We somehow never think of the parish council in a village as the

'State' and yet a parish council can be as helpful or as coercive as any government department. According to the political structure of a country the idea of the State varies its meaning. In a totalitarian state it means the Government. In Russia it is the Government and cannot be anything else. It is government of the people but neither by them nor for them. In England this is what it used to mean, with the addition that it included the 'governing classes'. Whigs and Tories and even Liberals were all found in the governing classes and, while their political views might be radically different, the social classes from which the leaders were drawn were the same. Government was a specialized activity, a game played by opponents who knew the rules while everyone else looked on. You went in for politics as you went into the Church or the army or the law.

The twentieth century in Britain and to some degree in all countries, except those under totalitarian regimes, has seen a gradual change in the idea and the structure of the 'State' which can be expressed in one phrase—the change from 'the Government' to 'society', i.e. the community as a whole. The idea of the State as a coercive body of politicians and government officials has given way to the more organic view of a society of all classes co-operating for the common good. This, of course, is not to be confused with the welfare state. The welfare state is only one step towards such a society. But the fact that 'society' is assuming more and more importance represents a radical change, although neither our choice of terms nor our general attitude has as yet caught up with it. It will be recognized on all sides that this is a change for the better, but there are certain corollaries which follow from it and which indicate that a new set of problems is on the way.

When the State meant the Government, the relationship between the State and the people was strictly 'political'. That is to say it was concerned with the distribution of power by which the community could act together. Vote by ballot, the franchise, the liberty of the individual, the balance between the legislative, the executive and the judicial organs of the State, the functioning of the press, the relation of the nation to other nations, are all examples of political questions. Nowadays, however, the State is concerned with far more than these, and with a different kind of question. I am writing this in the village of Hawarden where there is a library, a statue, a fountain and a castle each dedicated to the memory of William Ewart Gladstone. When I look at that massive regal figure I find it interesting to speculate what he would have thought of Parliament in our time solemnly discussing the price of cheese and the quality of beer—to take but two examples from the work of a recent session. The Midlothian campaign would have taken on a different aspect if such domestic issues had had to be included! In the library here are over fifty volumes of Gladstone's speeches and pamphlets, and I doubt if any of them at any point discusses the price of cheese. Today a whole realm of domestic and industrial life once thought to be outside 'politics' has now been brought within political discussion and political action. Yet if we are to consider 'society' as the ultimate reference of the term 'State' it is clear that everything which concerns the well-being of men in society is sooner or later bound to become the corporate concern of the community acting through its various agents—local and central, economic, political and cultural. It is one of the ironies of the present situation that the Communist slogan should represent the reorientation of political life in all progressive countries—'from each according to his capacity; to each according to his need'. There has never been a more worthy statement of the economic aims of government. Nevertheless all this has its disadvantages and there is a 'seamy side of progress'.[1] For all to accept responsibility for each involves a vast increase of bureaucracy, since these various services will not run themselves. There is consequently an increasing interference by the executive with the lives of citizens and a corresponding displacement of individual initiative. The present-day State has been called the 'New Leviathan'—the omnicompetent body which incorporates into itself all the lives in the nation which it serves. The 'State' can be a coercive authority equally under

[1] Elton Mayo, *The Social Problems of an Industrial Civilisation* (1945), chapter I.

a Socialist and under a Conservative regime. Indeed it may be even more coercive under Socialists because of the larger area of interests that are brought within its concern.

Americans often thank their stars that in a land of private enterprise these things cannot happen, but the welfare state is on the way to them also and private enterprise already is not so private, in the sense of uncontrolled, as it used to be. Nevertheless the prospect for all of us cannot but cause anxiety.

It is doubtful, however, whether what has been called the 'passing of Parliament' is the right term. What seems to be happening is that Parliament is taking on a new function, namely the protection of the individual against the administration. The one thing which our bureaucrats cannot face is that excellent remedy for social injustice, a 'question in Parliament'. Just before the war a farmer at a place called Crichel Down in Dorset had his land taken from him to be used as a bombing range. When the war was over he was not allowed to get it back because some minor officials had decided to hand it over to the Ministry of Agriculture. A question in Parliament set to work a vast machinery, including a commission, and in the long run justice was done. The lesson of Crichel Down has not been lost on the Civil Service.[1]

## 2 LAW AND JUSTICE

Clearly, therefore, the relations of Church and State have necessarily undergone a great change from what they were even half a century ago. It is not a question of a coercive government versus an ecclesiastical institution, nor is the only issue between them the determination of the limits of political obedience. It is rather the question how we are all to live together in a self-governing community inspired with concern for the good estate of all its members.

At this point there is a vital question to be asked. We have seen that the term 'Church' apparently means two things—the external institution and the invisible, ideal community—and that in Protestantism the second is regulative of the first. Is there

[1] R. Douglas Brown, *The Battle of Crichel Down* (1955).

in politics anything which corresponds to such an ideal in religion? Is there also an invisible ideal State regulative of the State on earth?

There is, and it is called Natural Law.

The State like the Church is an institution of an external order, and as such it can become a law unto itself and recognize no authority over itself either human or divine. That is what is meant by the doctrine of sovereignty. But it can also be acknowledged that the State, like the institutional Church, is constantly under judgement, not only with regard to the laws made by society itself, which is what we mean when we say that the law is above the State, but still more from this natural law which is implanted in the hearts of all men and was given to them at their birth. There are, as we have seen, states which function without any regard to any ideal beyond themselves, where the 'State' and the 'Government' are one and the same thing, while such ideas as 'society', 'democracy', 'liberty' and 'tolerance' are looked upon as hopelessly old-fashioned. While, however, we must certainly have regard to things as they are and be certain of the applicability of our use of the term 'State' to states in particular, we are nevertheless concerned here with the State 'in a free society'. Our primary concern therefore will be with the conception of the State that best fits into this context.

The State then is an external institution and it is also an ideal, and the ideal can be used as a sanction or as a challenge. The conception of an ideal community can provide justification for the State as it now is, or it can act as a rebuke, an inspiration or a challenge to what now is. There is thus a similarity in the functioning of the Church and of the State, but nevertheless there is an important difference between them. In the case of the Church the ideal and the actual are by definition mutually interdependent. The challenge—on either side—is as much part of the Gospel as the sanction. But as the most easily recognizable characteristic of the State is *power* some quite different factor has to come in to give direction to that power and if need be to mitigate it. The State in a free society is beneath and not above the law, and the law which thus governs it is not only what is called the 'law of the land' but also some 'unwritten charter' of which the law of the land seeks to be an expression. While, therefore, we have to consider only two factors on the side of the Church, namely the external institution and the ideal church, it would seem that in the case of the State there are three: namely, the Government, the law, which is above the Government, and 'natural law', which is above both. The law of the land cannot claim to be above the State in so far as it represents the interests of a separate group of officials, but only in so far as it upholds the rights and obligations of all citizens equally. The law of nations, however, was always equated with the law of nature, which was concerned with men as men irrespective of the state to which they belonged.

Perhaps an illustration will make this clear. In the South Africa Act of 1909 which determined the status of the Union there were what were called the 'entrenched clauses'. These, among other matters, had to do with the status of the African people within the Union. They were considered by the British Liberal Government of the time to provide an adequate guarantee that the rights of Africans, recognized by the British Government, would continue to be respected by the Union Government. It was, however, provided that these entrenched clauses could be abrogated, but only after adequate discussion by both houses of the South African parliament, and by a two-thirds vote of both houses. It was considered at the time that this would be likely to happen only where the status of the native was to be improved rather than made worse, for the latter to the minds of Liberal politicians was quite unthinkable.[1] However, the unthinkable, as so often in South African history, actually happened. The Malan Government, inspired by its doctrine of white racial superiority, determined to attack the entrenched clauses. The clauses were abrogated by vote of the lower house but the Supreme Court ruled the Act to be unconstitutional because it had not been passed by a two-thirds majority of *both* houses. The Government under Malan's successor then attacked both the Senate and the Supreme Court, and by

[1] See the speech by the Earl of Crewe in A. B. Keith, *British Colonial Policy, 1763–1917*, II, p. 35.

altering the membership of both they got their majority in both houses of Parliament, while an appeal to the Supreme Court against the Act was of course useless. No one could hold that it was not within the power of Parliament to do these things (and the present South African Government has never shrunk from a naked display of power), but so to alter the law as to make it a sanction of wrongdoing rather than a challenge against it created the uncomfortable feeling that some divine principle was being infringed. The law which was now theoretically above the State had been placed there not by any right of its own, and so was not an expression, but a violation, of natural law. The Government had deliberately made use of the law to perpetrate injustice. To say in defence, as they did, that this was a purely domestic issue was to show an incredible blindness to the universality of moral values. Where justice is at stake there are no domestic issues.

Emil Brunner in a notable book[1] draws a distinction between law and justice. The distinction is valid in the sense that one goes to court not, as many think, to get 'justice' but to get a verdict based on the law. But the distinction between law and justice is an important one for another reason. Justice is law *plus* mercy, and mercy has nothing to do with the sentence but rather with the way of arriving at it. The picture, however, that we usually have in our minds is somewhat different. The accused is tried according to the law and if guilty the appropriate punishment is discovered and declared. But, although he should get what he deserves, a plea for mercy is put forward in order that there may be a mitigation of the sentence. This situation appears also a good deal in theological thinking. God is the stern judge. We are condemned for our sins; but, although we deserve to be punished, Christ comes in to beg that we be let off. Both these positions are fundamentally immoral. To think of law in this way is to think of it as John Austin thought of it, namely as the decree of a law-giver who has his own reasons for what he does and can be as arbitrary as he chooses. The idea is that if you plead hard enough or have a friend at court you can avoid getting what you deserve. This has no

[1] *Justice and the Social Order* (1945).

relation whatever to justice and at times it even makes the law itself of no effect. In so far as positive law is striving towards justice it must—and does—take into account all the mitigating or aggravating circumstances, and the final decision accords with the situation as a whole. It is a common misunderstanding, however, which has dogged discussions both in politics and in theology and into which Brunner himself falls,[1] to look upon mercy as mitigating *justice*. Mercy can mitigate law, for laws can be unjust and so mercy is invoked to equate them with justice. But mercy itself is comprehended in justice.

## 3 NATURAL LAW

What then is this natural law to which the law of the State must conform? Hooker's rolling periods at once come to mind:

> Of Law there can be no less acknowledged than that her seat is the bosom of God, her voice the harmony of the world. All things in heaven and earth do her homage, the very least as feeling her care, and the greatest as not exempted from her power.[2]

Some may say that this is mysticism if not mere words, but when it is set against the actions of the South African Nationalists or against the mockery of political trials in Communist countries it is perfectly clear that it presents a very definite challenge to the powers that be.

Hooker, however, was not the originator of the idea. In Proverbs viii we have the personification of divine wisdom—'By me kings reign, and princes decree justice', and there are the still more famous words of Antigone in Sophocles' play when she justifies her deliberate breach of the king's commandment:

> These laws of yours were not ordained by God, nor did I ever think a mortal man such as you are could by a breath annul the unchangeable unwritten laws of heaven. *These* were not born today nor yesterday: they die not and none knoweth whence they sprang.[3]

Thus the validity or invalidity of a law depends not on the majority by which it is passed but by its conformity to standards of justice eternal in the heavens. It is part of human psychology

[1] *Op. cit.* p. 16. [2] *Laws of Ecclesiastical Polity* I, xvi. 8. [3] Lines 450–7.

to feel that in all serious human transactions the immortal gods are somehow concerned and it is as well to have them on one's side if possible. It is this appeal to the ideal order of things that has nerved the rebel to fight despite overwhelming odds against the established order and has sustained him in a prison cell or on the scaffold. On the other hand the sense of heaven on one's side has also kept men calm in times of wild anarchic revolution. The appeal can be made both by the reformer and by the guardian of things as they are—in one case as a challenge and in the other as a sanction. No man can be satisfied with a position which is its own justification: he must reach out and above himself in order to be in the right in other eyes than his own.

In England it is significant that we use the phrase 'the common law', as opposed to statute law, to indicate what these principles are that apparently have lodgement in the hearts of all men. If we ask what are these dictates of natural law, we can find a good statement of them in the Declaration of Human Rights in the United Nations Charter. It is accepted as axiomatic that we have a 'natural' right to life, liberty and security, a right to be recognized as equal before the law, to be held innocent until proved guilty, to have private property, to be free to discuss and assemble and to take part directly or indirectly in the government of our own country. Such rights as these are based on no positive enactments but are, as we should say, in the very nature of things. Accordingly a free society will give a greater place to natural law and the relations of Church and State will operate within the sphere which it has worked out.

The reader of the New Testament seeking for guidance in the practical matters of social and political life is often nonplussed at its absence. But behind the New Testament and taken for granted by it is the conception of natural law which was taken over from the ancient world and which gave a basis if not specific instructions for political and social conduct. When St Paul commended those Gentiles who though they 'have not the [Jewish] law, do by nature the things contained in the law',[1] he was in effect appealing

[1] Romans ii, 14.

to that law of nature which had been popularized by the Stoics. With the doctrine, however (and it has had a long and varied history), we are not here so much concerned. It is as an effective regulator of relationships that it comes into a consideration of Church and State.

Around all law there is a sort of mystical aura. Perhaps it is helped in Britain where wigs and gowns lend a touch of symbolism lacking in those places where justice is dispensed in shirt sleeves. But in earlier times there was something about the dispensation of the law which removed it altogether from the ordinary affairs of daily life. In his charge to the judges of Israel these words are put into the mouth of Moses: 'Ye shall not respect persons in judgement; but ye shall hear the small as well as the great; ye shall not be afraid of the face of man; *for the judgement is God's*.'[1] The existence of this natural law, which is here identified with the will of God, rests upon the fundamental nature of man as God created him. The sense of right and wrong (without affirming what things are right and what things are wrong) is part of human psychology, and the fact that we call the choices we make 'right' or 'wrong' indicates that they are not made entirely by expediency or casual preference. Thus the external acts of the State are constantly under judgement, and positive law—despite the fashion of these times in which we live—is constantly striving towards the perfect order of things, which is what we call justice. It is on a similar principle to this that the procedure of equity is based. Natural law therefore is a test of the justice and the validity of any particular law. The practical outcome of this is that allegiance to any government can be only conditional.

> Man is bound to obey secular rulers to the extent that the order of justice requires. For this reason if such rulers have no just title to power but have usurped it, or if they command things to be done that are unjust, their subjects are not obliged to obey them except perhaps in certain special cases where it is a matter of avoiding scandal or some particular danger.[2]

[1] Deuteronomy i. 17.

[2] Aquinas, *Summa Theol.* 2a 2ae, 104. 6, quoted by A. P. d'Entreves, *Natural Law* (1951), p. 43.

At the Reformation the idea of natural law disappeared from Protestant theology, except to be contradicted. The reformers and later, among others, Pascal, were sworn foes to that casuistry which interpreted 'natural law' in any way that was convenient and for which the user could not be held to account. It is interesting therefore to set over against this sentence from Aquinas another sentence from a Puritan writer, John Udall (died 1592), in a petition to Archbishop Whitgift: 'If the prince should command anything contrary to the word of God, it is not lawful for the subjects to rebel or resist, no, not so much as in thought: but with patience and humility to bear all the punishment laid upon them.' [1] Here is evidently a literal acceptance of Romans xiii—'the powers that be are ordained of God. Whosoever therefore resisteth the power, resisteth the ordinance of God'—beyond which there was no appeal.

The absence of natural law from the theology and preaching of the reformers deprived Protestantism of the necessary weapon with which to attack the economic exploitation of the poor both in the seventeenth century and in the days of the Industrial Revolution. They could not get beyond this text in Romans, and the wretchedness of the poor was put down to the mysterious workings of Providence. It was to the credit of the early Stuart kings that they had tried to mitigate the hardships of the enclosure acts, but the new men who profited by the industrial revolution of the eighteenth century were content to say with Pope

> Thus God and nature formed the general frame
> And bade self love and social be the same.[2]

## 4 THE SOCIAL CONTRACT

The thesis with which we began was that the State is ideal as well as actual and in both senses it can be used as a sanction to conduct or as a challenge. The idea of the ideal State is discovered under the operation of natural law, or the law of God. In so far

[1] J. Strype, *Life and Acts of John Whitgift* (Oxford, 1822), II, p. 98.
[2] See R. H. Tawney, *Religion and the Rise of Capitalism* (Penguin), p. 177.

as the State was simply the Government and the only issue was that of political obedience, this higher law took on a political colouring. It was assumed to be of the nature of a solemn contract entered into in prehistoric times whereby the people covenanted with one another to offer obedience to a ruler in return for protection. In other versions they made the covenant with the leader himself. The origin of the idea was not in history but in Scripture. It was a carrying-over into politics of the idea of the covenant God made with the people of Israel. When the fiery Welsh preacher Dr Price preached the sermon at the Old Jewry which called forth Burke's famous reply *Reflections on the French Revolution*, his argument for 'cashiering rulers for misconduct' was on the ground that where they had broken this mystical contract the people were loosed from the necessity of obedience. The theory was one way of getting out of the dilemma of non-resistance in which the Puritans had placed themselves. It is interesting to see, however, the hold that this theory still has on the minds of men. There is a recent restatement of it in Indian terms. Dr K. M. Pannikar holds that the citizen in a dependent society has the right of civil disobedience, because he has given no free moral assent to the regime, but in a self-governing society, since the citizen has conferred all his rights upon the State, all he can do is himself to refuse obedience and suffer the consequences, but on no account must he organize resistance even in a passive form.[1]

The theory of the social contract has long been exploded as a way of accounting for the origin of the State. It was an attempt to give concrete form to something which was a *feeling* rather than a fact, and the idea behind it—that there is some power behind the State to which the State itself owes homage—is relevant even for our own times. Lord Haldane in a famous address to the Bar Association of Montreal in 1913 gave to this feeling the German term *Sittlichkeit* and said: 'It resembles the morality of conscience in that it is enforced by no legal compulsion.' And he continued: 'It is this instinctive sense of what to do and what not to do in daily life and behaviour that is the source of liberty and

[1] *The State and the Citizen* (1956).

ease. And it is this instinctive sense of obligation that is the chief foundation of society.'

The rationalizing of these ideas took other forms besides the social contract. The most notable, of course, was the medieval Church-State for which the blue-print was drawn by Augustine. But this became more than a theory and like most ideologies which are worked out on paper and afterwards tried out in practice it was magnificent but it was not politics. With the setting-up of Charlemagne's empire the City of God came down from God out of heaven and all the mystical power that belonged to it was reinforced by political and even military action. The medieval Church-State has gone but the identification of the institution with the City of God has remained in Roman Catholicism and is considered to be the justification for coercion and for persecution.[1]

Now, however, that the State includes concern for wages, housing, health, industry, commerce, food, education and everything else, the relevance of a 'pattern in the mount' is not very easy to find. Even the most self-asserting despot would admit the existence of an overruling natural law although reserving to himself the right of interpretation. But what sort of pattern is there which can include social and economic factors as well as political? Socialism, Conservatism, the self-regulating market, Communism, all these and others have their own pattern and there is no agreement. The attempt to translate into concrete reality any one of them leads to the sort of conditions that prevail in Russia where ideologies have preference over people. Nationalization in Britain was believed to be able to bring down to earth the Socialist idea, but has it done so? Is there then no pattern to challenge things as they are?

It is here that we see the relevance of a penetrating remark by that great jurist Sir Henry Sumner Maine. 'Substantive law', he said, 'is secreted in the interstices of procedure.'[2] In other words, as cases arise and have to be dealt with as the circumstances

[1] Ronald Knox, *The Faith of Catholics* (1927), p. 241, See below, p. 90.

[2] *Early Law and Custom*, p. 389; commented upon by F. W. Maitland in *Forms of Action*, pp. 295 and 372.

allow, there emerge here and there principles which have a wider application and can be built up into some coherent system. It has been held against the League of Nations and the United Nations that they make the justice of a cause depend entirely on procedure.[1] If the right procedure is followed the case is more acceptable than if it is not. There is truth in this criticism, but it is not irrelevant to interpret it in the light of Maine's dictum. The United Nations organization has no laws which it can expound or which it could enforce even if it had them. It can only build up a code by dealing with cases as they come along, acting by general principles where possible, or taking cases on their merits where no general principles seem in advance to apply. The only line of action is by appeal to natural law, and if it be asked where it is, the answer is that it is in process of being revealed as we go along. In our time, even more than in the days of the Stoics, the law of nations (*jus gentium*) is equivalent to the law of nature (*jus naturale*).

The importance of this reference to natural law rests in the fact that the Church is no more free from it than the State. If the State is no longer just the Government but society itself, it is clear that when we speak of the Church we are talking about people every one of whom also belongs to the State. When the State was just the Government it could and did stand for a group of officers quite distinct from those of the institutional Church. But in a free society this is no longer so. Christians do not lay aside their obligations under natural law simply because they also come under the law of Christ, any more than citizens are exempt from natural law in obeying the law of the land. This materially affects Church and State relations, for an undue adherence to what is believed to be the law of the Church may turn out to be an offence against justice and mercy, and may drive out all natural feelings of good will and tolerance towards other members of the human family and thereby weaken the structure of a free society.

[1] H. A. Smith, *The Crisis in the Law of Nations* (1947), p. 84. See below, p. 179.

## CHAPTER V

# THE WHOLE MAN

### I TOTALITARIANISM TRUE AND FALSE

When we examine our definitions of the terms 'free society', 'Church' and 'State', we shall notice that they have one factor in common. This is a regard for persons as something that takes priority over a regard for theories, institutions or property. If, behind the Church as we see it in the form of a denomination, there is the ideal Church to which all sincere Christians belong, such an ideal Church clearly cannot be described as Anglican, Roman, Presbyterian or by the name of any other specific denomination, any more than it can be described as American, European, African or by the name of any other country, race or language. The Epistle to Diognetus, written possibly as far back as the third century, gives a notable description of the Church in this extra-territorial sense:

> The distinction between Christians and other people consists neither in country nor language nor customs. For they do not dwell in cities apart from other men nor do they have any strange vocabulary nor do they lead a peculiar kind of life. Yet while living in Greek and foreign cities and following local customs they nevertheless also show forth a wonderful and unusual type of citizenship of their own. They inhabit their own fatherlands, but as if sojourners in them. They share all things as citizens and suffer all things as strangers. Every foreign country is their fatherland and every fatherland is a foreign country. In short what the soul is in the body so are Christians in the world.[1]

The first chapter of the First Epistle to the Corinthians shows the robust attitude of St Paul to the denominational question as it had arisen in his time. There were contentions among Christians, some saying they were of Paul, others of Cephas, others of Apollos and others, simply 'of Christ'. The Apostle recalls them to their common loyalty to Christ, 'He that glorieth, let him glory in the

[1] §§ 5 and 6.

Lord'. It is men as men, men as they are in the presence of God, shorn of all adventitious titles and associations but not shorn of individual virtues and abilities that are the concern of this universal, invisible Church, and it is in this context that we have to consider it.

Similarly with the State. Its fundamental concern is with people and this is indicated by the growing emphasis on 'society' over against a governing class. Where this concern, however, is subordinated to the demands of a party, whether Communist, Socialist, Liberal, Catholic or Conservative, the State becomes inorganic, impersonal and authoritarian, the preserve of an official clique, and the people have no interest in the laws except to obey them. This may happen even under an apparently 'democratic' government as well as under a dictatorship, the only difference being that such a government would justify itself on the ground that it owes its position to free election by the people, while a dictatorship would justify itself on the ground that it knows the people's interests better than the people do themselves. But the ideal State is the embodiment of a concern for men and women as such, irrespective of class or party. And it is only where concern for people is the overriding consideration of *both* Church and State that there is the possibility of a 'free society'.

## 2 CHURCH, STATE AND PEOPLE

Where people are concerned we must remember that human personality functions as a whole. The three aspects of the self—body, mind and spirit—are not independent of one another any more than intellect, emotion and will are independent. There is continual mutual influence, and fully to understand any one element or activity requires a reference to all the others.

Accordingly in considering the relations of persons in a free society we need to concern ourselves with the whole man. His personality is not fully regarded if we take into account only his physical needs or his intellectual ability or his spiritual sensitiveness. He may on occasion ignore any or all of these; for while they are all, so to speak, necessary components of a personality the mysterious 'self' which governs all our activities may decide that, for some greater good, one or more of these may have to be sacrificed. Yet even here the 'self' is affected by its decision to enter into life maimed. To ignore the physical side of life is to provide an imperfect instrument for the carrying out of intellectual or spiritual purpose. To stultify the intellect and to turn a blind eye to evidence is to reduce spiritual sensitiveness to a point where ignorance and sin merge into one another. To carry on life with no regard for spiritual values is to put everything at the mercy of the corrosive intellect or of the animal passions and is the most serious deprivation of all. The history of mankind provides innumerable examples of all three kinds of deliberately impoverished lives.

A mistaken idea of what constitutes sacrifice in the Christian sense has led to the cult of the maimed life, even when neither the eye nor the hand has been the occasion of stumbling. It has been somehow assumed that to be maimed is in itself a virtue and therefore it must be deliberately sought after. Some types of monasticism represent this attitude and reckon to themselves for righteousness a deprivation artificially created. The early Church had to take strict measures against a growing habit of rushing into martyrdom, so seductive was the tendency to equate deprivation with holiness. Fundamentalists, both Catholic and Protestant, have shown an almost eager willingness to decry the intellect and have not scrupled to identify orthodoxy with ignorance. All these attitudes seem to rest on the assumption that the part is of more value than the whole.

When these partial expressions of personality become the special concern of the rival institutions of Church and State the harm that follows might be very considerable. But this allocation of offices whereby the Church exercises authority in spiritual things while the State is supreme in things temporal is quite unworkable, because we are dealing with the same people all the time and their personalities cannot be so divided. How is the line to be drawn between what is spiritual and what is temporal? In English history it was drawn with confident firmness in the ordinance of William the Conqueror, while Henry II's attempt was frustrated by the murder of Becket. But it has been a problem all down the ages and in every country.

This division, however, has not been the only attitude taken up by these two authorities. Concern for the 'whole man' has been exhibited by both Church and State, but in very different ways, some of them most unfortunate. For there is a right and wrong totalitarianism. The wrong kind seeks to bring every activity of human life under the control of the one institution. The other kind seeks to bring the whole of life under one regulative principle. Both types have been at work in relations between Church and State.

It has been the perpetual dream of many Christians to go back to the medieval system when apparently the Church controlled every side of life, spiritual, economic, political and social. This religious totalitarianism, which was an attempt to carry out in practice the ideas of Augustine's *City of God*, worked no better than the division between institutions. It would indeed have required a legion of supermen to carry it out and the authorities of the Church were anything but that. It was given up even in theory with the triumph of the national State. The national State in its turn in both Europe and America tried to keep its hold over its citizens and prescribe for them in every particular, but even on the national level the system was unworkable. Human nature is refractory material for planners.

Our modern totalitarian regimes have been a throw-back to the medieval system, aided this time by all the instruments of coercion that modern science can supply. In the Middle Ages the effective unit of social structure was the village, and the life of the village was based directly on the land. Consequently there was a certain homogeneity of life right across Europe. Feudalism was not greatly different in England from what it was in France and Germany and other lands. This homogeneous system had a long life, and after it was given up as a system it persisted at the back of men's minds as an idea of something in itself desirable. It fits in so well with that trait in human nature which makes us all like to be together of one heart and mind. The medieval villagers under the control of the lord of the manor and the parish priest lived alike and thought alike and worshipped alike. And those who have a taste for uniformity, especially under religious auspices, naturally experience a kind of romantic nostalgia for such an arrangement. Moreover it provides a specious justification for the use of power to bring about so desirable an end. This we have seen in recent times in totalitarian states, in Nazi Germany, Italy, Spain and Russia. It is an attempt to impose the homogeneity of an agricultural community upon communities that are highly industrialized. This is a recognition of the 'whole man' which does violence to the very persons in whose presumed interest the system is set up.

Under the feudal system the life of every man was governed by his status in the community. If his life was controlled at every point by some outside authority, at any rate he knew where he stood, and as a person he had his place, however humble, in the body politic. The opposite of this system came in with the Industrial Revolution when status gave way to contract. We shall have to consider this in another context shortly but meanwhile we can note the radical difference between the two. Under a system of status it is the man who matters even if he is a serf or a cottager. Under contract it is the man's labour alone that matters. Labour is a commodity to be bought and sold, and the buyer has no interest in the seller as a person. In industry and commerce *laissez-faire* became the recognized policy and the gospel of work, each man for himself, became the prevailing temper. The Church gave its blessing to this attitude and was content with an outward conformity to its own recognized standards of personal belief and conventional behaviour.

It would seem that today with a return to State action in every department of life the State is taking upon itself the tasks that the medieval Church-State sought to perform but for which it lacked ability. We must be careful here, however, to remember that the State nowadays is not the same as the Reformation State. It is society as a whole acting through its official institutions. It is also as much local as it is central, and in so far as it is local it is also to some extent worked by the voluntary services of the 'great unpaid' in local government and local justice. We have not therefore that fear of the State that our forefathers had. What we are concerned about is whether the instruments of communal action are those best suited for the purpose and whether because of so much communal action the individual citizen is having fair treatment. We are moving from contract to a new form of status, although both thought and action in economic relationships seem still to presuppose the continued existence of the old form of contract. Nevertheless a regard for persons necessarily involves a recognition of status. Labour should neither be bought nor refused, neither offered for sale nor withdrawn from sale, as if it were simply a commodity.

At bottom, therefore, our concern is with the whole man, and the distribution of that concern amongst private enterprise, voluntary groups and the government is the real problem before us. The fact that all these agencies must work together means that they must all share the same common concern if we are to have a free society. The arbitrary domination of one over the others is not to be tolerated. Status, however, in our modern society is different from that of the Middle Ages. It is not something fixed by custom or by law and rigidly applied. It is a social expression of mutual good will, appreciation, loyalty and co-operation, and therefore it is impossible to have it unless there is a recognition of obligation. The idea of 'rights' is as alien to this situation as it would be within a family.

Where a situation depends on good will rather than on legal enactment the guarantee of its successful working rests in the character of the people concerned. It is therefore to be expected that a primary duty of the Church is to foster that type of character which makes for good citizenship. The Church must be the conscience of the nation, for, more than other institutions, it is concerned with ultimate values and the true destiny of man. The conscience of the nation, however, must be concerned with more than belief and individual behaviour. It will never be able to affect national life if these are its sole concern, unless we give a far wider connotation to both 'belief' and 'behaviour' than is usual. If belief is no more than intellectual assent we have Scriptural warrant for the view that the devils also believe.[1] It is not, however, a question of adding to intellectual assent some external action, as if these two were somehow separate, but it is rather a development of assent into commitment. This is a fashionable term nowadays and it is worth noticing that it is the middle term between thought and action. The separation between thought and action requires a suitable motive, and it is commitment that makes the action appropriate to the thought and also gives it the right motive. It is the absence of commitment in the situation referred to in Matthew vii that gives point to the otherwise 'hard saying' of Jesus: 'Many will say to me in that day, Lord, Lord, have we not prophesied in thy name? and in thy name have cast out devils? and in thy name done many wonderful works? And then will I profess unto them, I never knew you: depart from me, ye that work iniquity.'

The question arises—What is it commitment *to*? Certainly not to an intellectual proposition, for a set of words is altogether inadequate as an expression of the sentiment of loyalty. Certainly not to a type of behaviour, for this might mean no more than conformity. In the Christian way of thinking it is commitment to Christ and to his way of life. In the book of Acts 'the Way' was the earliest name for the Christian Church and the Gospels were illustrations of the origin of the Way. The Way involves all the factors that make up one's life—physical, intellectual, political, economic, social and religious. It involves service but not on the Rotarian basis of 'service before self' (a flattering unction if ever there was one!) but on Christian terms, that is, service to mankind through service to God. And it must be capable of expression in a thought-out belief and in educated emotions. All these are involved in what is meant by the 'whole man' for which both Church and State in a free society have concern.

It is on the physical side that life first manifests itself, and by its

[1] Epistle of James ii. 19.

dissolution sets free the spirit of man from bodily circumstance. To isolate this side of life, however, and to make of it the central concern as in a cultus such as Christian Science, is to ignore the composite nature of human personality and also the manner in which individual lives use their diversity of gifts in the service of the community. It is surely true that Christianity is concerned with spiritual healing but this does not necessarily mean that the normal, proper and most Christian way of procedure is through direct action. Theoretically if prayer can cure disease it ought to be able to stave off death. This indeed was Mrs Eddy's firm belief and the story of the effort of this latter-day Mrs Partington to sweep back the waves of mortality does not make very edifying reading.[1] Why, however, should it be assumed that God works on disease only in the direct way? Are there not even more effective indirect ways? It is noticeable that within the last eighty years medical science, better standards of nutrition and improved public health have added no less than twenty years to the normal expectation of human life. That is to say that because of these services a large number of people are still alive who on earlier calculations would have died. Faith is not the only thing that wards off disease. In a free society the Church with its spiritual methods and the community with its other relevant agencies of public health work together in their concern for the well-being of the same people. Just as the true agency of evangelism is the whole church in fellowship and worship, so also the true agency for the well-being of society is the community as a whole. Where one member suffers, all the members suffer with it. This I take to be the spiritual basis of the welfare state.

If the physical side is the concern of both Church and State, so also must be the economic side of life and its social structure. Here, however, as we have already seen, many problems arise. Christian social ethics took their rise in small communities or in towns which, like all towns down to the eighteenth century, preserved the village *ethos*, and it is therefore not surprising that it is extremely difficult to see just where Christianity can fit into

[1] E. F. Dakin, *Mrs Eddy: the Biography of a Virginal Mind* (1929).

a highly complex society like our own. To state the problem, of course, is not to solve it, but there have been many attempts at solution before the problem has even been properly stated.

## 3 CHRISTIANITY AND OTHER RELIGIONS

What guarantee have we that religion will be either a sanction or a challenge to social and economic life? May it not be that it is a compensation for the many difficulties in which we find ourselves? The hard word for this is 'escapism', and it is a very common attitude. When a man is seeking in his frustration to attach himself to some authoritarian religion, it may quite easily be due not to conviction but to weariness. The Roman Church records a large number of intellectuals who in the last thirty years have come over to Rome, and their professions of faith gathered together in the several volumes of *The Road to Damascus* witness to the intense relief with which they have found themselves safe in the bark of St Peter. Similar testimonies can be found in the Fundamentalist groups. There is not a great deal to indicate that they look on this experience as any other than an end in itself. If, however, religion is meant to come down into the arena of life and help a man and help a community to grasp this sorry scheme of things entire and see how it can be made more tolerable, it cannot be looked upon as a compensation for the penalty of having to live here at all. Yet apart altogether from the variants of Christianity that make their appeal to the frustrated there is also an evangelistic spirit being shown by other religions. It is rather a sad comment on Christian missions that Dr Ambedkar, the leader of the Indian 'untouchables' just before he died became a convinced Buddhist because he felt that Buddhism alone had something relevant to say to the cause for which he had given his life. Buddhism has made headway in England and is represented by an interesting group of people including an eminent Q.C. Islam has made considerable progress here also. These two religions have many attractive features. They do appear, especially Islam, much more *possible* religions than Christianity. Both the inwardness of Buddhism and the externalism of Islam represent standards which can be understood and very largely achieved by a large number of people. The strenuous nature of Christianity, with its doctrine of sin and redemption, is for many people, especially those of an intellectual type, more of an affront than a challenge. For some people the continual demand that it makes for new adventure in personal living and in social regeneration adds to the burden they already have to bear from things as they are. To have the benefits of Christianity without the constant challenge to higher things is for many people an admirable compromise. The relations of Church and State then sink into the relations between two institutions; the purposes of each being the concern of nobody but its own members. It leaves the State to go to the devil in its own way if it chooses and it regards as impossible any change in human nature which will bring a new free society. It is just this attitude which has caused the ineffectiveness of the Orthodox Church. It has concerned itself with the minutiae of theological speculation and ritual. (An Anglican bishop once said to me concerning them, 'They are the people who understand clothes.') Western Christianity with all its faults has had a more serious concern for the salvation of men and the redemption of society.

## CHAPTER VI

# THE WHOLE COMMUNITY

### 1 SOCIETY PAST AND PRESENT

In the framing of a Christian sociology as in the consideration of relations between Church and State, not only the whole man but also the whole of society is concerned.

To this principle I wish to give a special reference. We have already accepted the idea that the social, economic, intellectual, political and spiritual sides of life have all to be taken care of in a free society and that they are every one of them the concern both of the Gospel and of the State. But 'society' is more than the community of people at present alive. We cannot think of it as a whole unless we pay regard to the past and the future as well as the present. We ourselves are at the middle stage, and we cannot therefore rightly assess even ourselves without reference to whence we have come and whither we go.

### 2 THE GRACE OF ANCESTRY

Reference to the past of society means neither sentimentality nor ancestor worship. But it does mean three very important things that both Christians and citizens require for a full appreciation of their gifts and their vocation. These three are a sense of dignity, an enlargement of experience, and a discipline of the spirit.

The sense of not being a thing of yesterday but of having an ancestry so that we ourselves and the society to which we belong are recognized as part of a larger whole has in itself much of the material for self-respect. Self-respect is a most curious sentiment. It looks as if it had to do only with the present, with the man as he now appreciates himself to be. This, however, is more characteristic of the self-made man who is very proud of his creator, for self-respect is something quite different. It implies a standard and the record of acceptance of that standard from times past. It is a recognition that we are not entirely to be accounted for by what we are ourselves, but that there is something else to be considered, something which is both within us and yet not within us at all. Ancestry does this for a man, but we must not confine ancestry to distinguished parentage, for this can be a possession of very few. We all had ancestors. No matter with what period of history or indeed of pre-history we concern ourselves, our direct ancestor was present at that time. He was contemporary with Napoleon and Charlemagne and St Paul. What matters in the reckoning of the world is not whether we had ancestors or not, but who they were. Can we remember them?

I suggest that one far more realistic and effective way of having ancestors is by adoption.

A boy about to be sent to a boarding school may be completely indifferent as to which school he goes to. He is not committed to any. But once he has accepted a school he becomes at once vitally committed. All that ever went on in that school in the past becomes his own responsibility and he will stoutly defend events and practices as his own although they were there long before he was born and he himself has heard of them only within a matter of a few weeks. There is something about human beings which responds to this sort of thing. Men are continually adopting groups to which they can belong, and what is adopted is the past of these groups as well as the present. The man who has no past to belong to is indeed a poor creature. It was one of the things noticeable about the early Gentile Christians that although not many mighty, not many noble, were called, they acquired a patent of nobility by their adoption into a society whose beginnings were believed to go back to the creation of the world. People with an ancestry such as that found that they were indeed 'kings and priests unto God': they could hold their heads up in any company and not be ashamed. And this dignity has been observed in humble working folk of our own acquaintance. Unknown to the world, with no physical ancestry to be proud of, they have been put by their Christian profession into a long historical succession. This indeed is the spiritual principle of aristocracy, and all God's children were intended to be aristocrats.

This is at once an enlargement of experience. We can have experience in two ways—directly, as it happens to us, indirectly, as it happens to those whom we accept as our representatives. Our own experience is limited to our opportunities and to the measure of our native ability to make use of them. But as members of a society we vastly increase the range of our experience. History is to the community what experience is to the individual, and to be put into a historical succession through our membership of a society is clearly to enlarge our experience.

Enlargement of experience, however, brings with it certain necessary and acceptable limitations. To belong to a society means accepting not only the rules but also the *mores* of that society. Thus there are certain things one may not do because they are not the sort of thing done by people in that sort of society. To accept the enlargement of experience without accepting the discipline that goes with it is not really possible. There is no doubt a caricature of this whole attitude in the 'old school tie' theory, but let us remember that the exaggeration of an attitude or the abuse of it is no reflexion on the attitude itself. It is noticeable that all grammar schools and more and more secondary modern schools equip their scholars with blazers with coats of arms on the pockets. It is more difficult to let down the school if you happen to be wearing its uniform.

It has been a great error on the part of organized Labour to look on this sort of thing simply as the badge of organized capital. It has nothing whatever to do with capital or labour or snobbery or social climbing. It is part of the psychology of mankind. What things we are proud of in the past will no doubt vary from person to person, but in the long run they will be those things which we should like to see continued in the present and which have survival value for the future. In the Christian scheme of things the past, or what is often curiously called 'the Church triumphant', is an integral part of our heritage. It provides both enlargement of experience and the discipline that comes from it.

This great psychological benefit is no doubt destroyed if the past is looked upon simply as something dead and inert, to be copied slavishly but not to be put out to use and developed. The past is here with us in the present and it is no compliment to our forefathers to wrap up in a napkin the result of their labours which they have handed down to us. We can perhaps get the matter in the right perspective if we remember that we ourselves are building up a 'past' for those who come after us. We should ask ourselves how we should like our own work to be treated. We do not treat our political heritage as static; so why should our religious heritage be treated in this way? It is no doubt a check on our own extravagances as well as something to be proud of, but it is also there to be used, and its use often indicates how much or how little we esteem it.

When Lord Baldwin, a former Prime Minister of Great Britain, died, Parliament was as usual adjourned as a tribute to his memory. A speech of appreciation of the dead leader was then made by the Prime Minister, Mr Attlee, and he was followed by the leader of the Opposition, Mr Winston Churchill, and by the leader of the Liberal party. Then to the surprise of the House there arose Mr Gallagher, one of the two Communist members of Parliament, and, according to the *Spectator*, he made the most moving speech of all. While naturally and totally disagreeing with Lord Baldwin's politics he nevertheless paid a warm tribute to him as a Parliamentarian who had kept a high standard in the House to which Mr Gallagher himself was proud to belong. I narrated this little incident to an American friend who was declaiming violently against Communists and suggested that it indicated a better way of dealing with Communists than the American method of persecution. His reply impressed me. He said that no doubt Gallagher was a Communist but he was also a Briton who had behind him six centuries of parliamentary government, and it was impossible for a man to be untrue to that sort of heritage whether he was a Communist or not. My friend then went on to say that so many American Communists were only one generation American and their background was quite different from that of Mr Gallagher.

## 3 THE CLAIM OF POSTERITY

As with the past and the present so also with the future. If society as a whole has to be considered in the relations of Church and State the future cannot be left to take care of itself. Here is the criticism of all quick political decisions based on expediency. A century from now it may possibly be found that one of the most unfortunate events in the history of the world was the Balfour Declaration of 1917 giving as a national home for the Jews lands which were already occupied by families who had been there for generations. Perhaps another will be the Yalta Conference at which Churchill and Roosevelt gave a free hand to Russia in the East in exchange for a free hand to themselves in the West. These two events were each decided upon in an hour of crisis, and each had its desired immediate result, but the consequences have been disastrous. It may be argued, of course, that there might have been no future at all for the Western nations if these desperate measures had not been taken at the time, a judgement which no one can either prove or gainsay. But they have both been lessons to indicate that it is possible to mortgage the future for the benefit of the present and to ignore the fact that everyone of us is only a trustee and not an owner of anything over which we have temporary control.

The future of society, like the past, is here in the present. It cannot be cut off and considered in isolation as if it were a purely theoretical consideration. It is present in a context of development. We are often misled in our appreciation of the past by thinking of it as utterly different from the present. This is partly a matter of unfamiliar costume and language in the case of our forefathers and partly due to our obsession with scientific progress. It is assumed that if our ancestors came back they would be utterly bewildered by the marvels of the intervening ages—stone roads, railways, steamships, electricity in all its many forms, wireless and television. Perhaps that is true, but perhaps also they would not take so long in adapting themselves as we think. They would find underneath all our present civilization that men still worked and played, ate and drank, got married and had children, suffered disappointment and frustration, had their joys and achievements, had diseases, old age came upon them, and they died. The fundamental experiences and problems are there all the time. And as it is so for ourselves in our relations to the past, so it will be in the future in relation to ourselves. What the men of the future will appreciate in us will not be our wireless and television but rather the sort of success we make of the art of living. Above all they will be most concerned with our success or otherwise in knitting together the human family. That is a problem which each generation hands on to the one that comes after it, and it is indeed the common factor in history. How can we live together? How can the immense resources of the world be made available for the whole of the world's people? How far can we extend the principle 'each for all and for each'? In regard to these matters, past, present and future are all together here and now, and they are all concerned in the solution of all our problems.

If these things are matters for society they are equally matters for the Church. The development of each of these two institutions is continually making a contribution to that ideal invisible State and that ideal invisible Church which are the pattern for those on earth. There is a germ of truth in the Catholic theory of the 'treasury of merits'. The institution is vitally important because it is only through the institution that we can, as it were, have anything to put in the bank to be drawn upon by later generations. But the institution is important also because it takes care of the person in that brief period of time during which he and it are both on the earth together. In a sense the institution is different in every generation, because each generation is different. But what is of worth in that generation will be preserved through the invisible society for the future. Browning is not very fashionable nowadays, but his *Abt Vogler* shows a firmer grasp of this fundamental truth than is shown by many of our contemporaries.

All we have willed or hoped or dreamed of good shall exist,
Not its semblance, but itself. No beauty nor good nor power
Whose voice has gone forth, but each survives for the melodist
When eternity affirms the conception of an hour.

## CHAPTER VII

# THE RATIONALE OF PROGRESS

### I VICTORY AND PERSUASION

A further principle we have to observe in a free society is that in personal relations victory is of no value in itself.

> He that complies against his will
> Is of his own opinion still.

This couplet from *Hudibras*, so self-evident as to be a platitude, would, if taken to heart, work a mighty revolution not only in Communist countries but everywhere. We live in an age when victory is more esteemed than truth, and violence is held to be the easiest and quickest way to bring peace. This is not unknown in the Christian Church and Augustine's misapplication of the text 'Compel them to come in'[1] has been used again and again to justify the use of force against heretics. Monsignor Ronald Knox in his book *The Faith of Catholics* states the case in modern terms.[2] Nevertheless it is self-condemned, for it is the parent of hypocrisy and of almost every other unedifying attitude.

We come back, therefore, to the Church's central symbol, the Cross. As a historical event it was the grim culmination of a life of love which was always willing to believe the best, was always patient, always hopeful, and went down in defeat and death rather than compel any man to accept his way of life. That life was celebrated by St Paul in his first letter to the Corinthians, chapter xiii. But the Crucifixion of Jesus and all its associations have had the effect of exhibiting to men all down the ages the principle on which God rules the world both in creation and also in redemption. Life comes only from death or the willing risk of it and this natural law was seen to be operative also in the spiritual world. Accor-

[1] Luke xiv. 23. See Augustine, *Epistle* 93, 2, 5.

[2] See below, p. 45.

dingly this principle has been taken up into theology and around it has gathered all that we know or need to know about God's relations to man and man's relations to his fellow-men. We know this principle to be true, it is the organon of man's redemption, but in actual practice in our relationships we cannot help ourselves and if we have at hand the means of coercion we can so easily take the short cut and convince ourselves that the end justifies the means.

This, however, is not the only reason for the use of persuasion rather than violence. It is a psychological fact that success of any kind tends to have an adverse effect on the human spirit. It is a most frequent source of pride, and pride means the ruin of happy relationships between persons. Where it has been gained at someone else's expense it creates resentment and bitterness and bids goodbye to any reconciliation while the sense of triumph is present. We have already seen how sensitive Archbishop Davidson was to this sort of thing, and how he feared the aftermath of a forcible settlement of the General Strike.[1] Even the slight sense of superiority that comes from having a person in your debt is dangerous—dangerous to you and humiliating to him. It is one of the many good features of the book of Deuteronomy that it so well recognizes this fact and deals with it in detail.[2]

But curiously enough a victory gained by force is also very unsatisfying to the human conscience of the victor. He *knows* that it is wrong and he tries to justify the result on grounds other than that of naked force. This is surely why in Communist countries they attempt to give their vicious treatment of opponents some show of decency by seeking to have 'confessions'. It may be asked why, since in any case they intend to murder their victims, the persecutors should insist on confession. The reason is not far to seek and it sheds a very interesting light on the working of the human mind. This procedure has the appearance of fair-mindedness and flatters the conscience. Even the worst of men feel the need to be in good standing with a conscience however

[1] Above, pp. 9, 27.

[2] E.g. 'When thou dost lend thy brother any thing, thou shalt not go into his house to fetch his pledge. Thou shalt stand abroad and the man to whom thou dost lend shall bring out the pledge abroad unto thee.' Deuteronomy xxiv. 10, 11.

depraved. They may make their bed in hell, but behold, God is there, unrecognized.

Persuasion, however, does not mean giving in to wrongdoing. It is the weakness of certain types of pacifism that justice and injustice are made to appear both alike. This might possibly be excused if oneself alone is concerned and if this happens to be one's own principle of action, but where other people are concerned it is not so clear. Where violence seems to be the only possible means of restraint it seems justifiable to use it, but everything depends on what happens next. A remark of Abraham Lincoln is apposite. He declared that the only value of victory was to get the other man into a position where reconciliation became possible. The shocking period of 'Reconstruction' which followed the American Civil War after Lincoln's death shows the evil result of victory for victory's own sake.

Does then persuasion mean the willingness to compromise? Yes and no. In the American Civil War compromise between those who stood by the Union and those who stood for the right of secession was clearly impossible, but not all cases are so clear cut. Compromise has been defined by the cynic as doing what you know to be wrong in order to persuade someone else to do what *he* knows to be wrong. A good deal of political manœuvring is undoubtedly of this kind. There is, however, a legitimate kind of compromise, which is the consideration of the circumstances of a special case in the application of a general law. Compromise indeed is a means whereby the law can be used to maintain justice. The Lord Chief Justice of England (Lord Goddard) some time ago gave a notable illustration of this procedure. A young soldier was tried by court martial for the murder of another in camp. It was made clear that the murdered man was a notorious bully and a most undesirable character. He had bullied and maltreated this youth beyond endurance and in a scuffle he was killed. This was technically murder and the military court treated it as such. The Lord Chief Justice himself, however, pointed out that in the circumstances this was a questionable decision and had the case come before a civil court the judge's recommendation would have been for a verdict of manslaughter.[1] A similar case in literature is Herman Melville's story of Billy Budd, whose action was the immediate but not the ultimate cause of the death of the ship's bully.

What compromise amounts to, when properly used, is the recognition of the human element in the situation and a regard for it as well as for the principles that are involved. It is this which prevents the taking of a short cut, and of course violence is always a short cut. There is an admirable idea enshrined in the phrase 'a stay of execution', for while possession of the means of coercion allows and even suggests immediate action, the desire to do justice necessarily involves a breathing space and time for consideration.[2] Jesus urged his followers not to go to law if they could avoid it but to forgive the offending brother until seventy times seven. Justice is done more surely by forgiveness and reconciliation than by victory. This is an axiom in Britain with regard to matrimonial cases at law, many of which are settled by discussion in a judge's private room and never come into court at all.

So far we have had in mind mainly individual action. But what of corporate action? Is there no place for majority rule? Are we to decry the value of victory to a political party at the polls or to some worthy cause in Parliament or elsewhere? What else, for instance, would have put an end to the scandal of the Contagious Diseases Acts but a victory over the forces in Parliament that justified them?[3]

Here again circumstances alter cases. Victory in war is quite a different thing from victory in Parliament. If no pressure is put on the opponents, and if they have an equal right to try, if they can, to turn their minority into a majority (admittedly two very big 'ifs'), victory is simply the recognition of the fact that most

[1] *The Times*, Law Report, 19 November 1956.

[2] We shall see later, pp. 157f., how the Mosaic law was very sensitive in this matter of allowing time for reflexion.

[3] These were Acts that arose out of the high incidence of venereal disease in the British army in the days after the Crimean War. They gave authority to any policeman to haul *any* woman into the police station and compel her to have a medical examination. They were withdrawn as the result of the uncompromising and intensive campaign of Josephine Butler and her friends.

people are on your side. This is a patent fact which cannot be gainsaid and will be accepted equally by any normal persons whether they win or lose. But victory in war is an entirely different thing. Men have been killed on both sides, the issues at stake were such that the risk of death was (rightly or wrongly) looked upon as worth taking, and when the war is over there is left in the vanquished a sense of humiliation and bitterness. This no doubt cannot be helped, but, as has been said before, it can only be justified if it immediately opens the way to reconciliation. The Southerners at the end of the American Civil War were treated by the North not as fellow Americans but almost as outcasts and the bitterness of that period is at the root of the Negro problem today.

The Quakers are an illustration of the opposite principle. For three hundred years they have carried on their church without ever having taken a vote. After discussion of an issue the clerk of the meeting, if it appears to him that the time is appropriate, rises and reads out what he believes to be the 'sense of the meeting'. In most cases the insight of an experienced man will cause this to be accepted as such, but if it is not, the issue is discussed further, usually after an interval of silent meditation. This no doubt takes a long time, but there are no bitter emotions at the end, for unanimity has been reached. Time is not the primary consideration and therefore a postponement is always possible if there happens at first to be a deadlock. It is a tribute to the prestige of this small denomination, which more than any other is willing to let itself be ruled by the Spirit, that this procedure is more and more favoured by other groups where religious questions are concerned. There is always something unhappy about majority rule in these cases. If the Church in the past had had more regard for the feelings of minorities there would scarcely have been the confusion in the world of religion that there is today.

## 2 THE UNITED NATIONS' DECLARATION OF HUMAN RIGHTS

Here then are a number of principles which are offered as the basis of a Christian sociology, as ideals which can be workable in practice. We might consider at this stage how far they coincide with the Declaration of Human Rights which is part of the Charter of the United Nations.

In the text which was adopted by the General Assembly at Paris on 10 December 1948 there is a preamble of seven clauses followed by thirty articles. It is a document worthy of study and comparison with the American Declaration of Independence. In neither document is there any reference to religious faith, although the name of God does appear once in the American preamble, and yet the effectiveness of the statements depends entirely upon the spiritual values believed in and acted upon by the peoples concerned. The United Nations' Declaration keeps in mind the events of the Second World War and in effect its declaratory clauses represent a positive statement to balance the disregard of human rights by the Germans and Japanese. Its opening clause is as follows: 'Whereas recognition of the inherent dignity and of the equal and inalienable rights of all members of the human family is the foundation of freedom, justice and peace in the world', and it continues: 'Whereas disregard and contempt for human rights have resulted in barbarous acts which have outraged the conscience of mankind,' etc. This document was signed by Russia—a fact which, as they say, gives one 'furiously to think'. This signature is important, however, because it shows the weakness of any paper agreement when there is no agreement on standards of conduct, just as, conversely, the Holy Alliance of 1816 showed its weakness by using religious language for proposals that were in themselves the very opposite of religious.

Article 1 declares that '...all human beings are born free and equal in dignity and rights. They are endowed with reason and conscience and should act towards one another in a spirit of brotherhood.' From this the Declaration goes on to specify what are 'human rights' as well as specifying what are human wrongs (such as slavery and torture). The rights are those to life, liberty and security (3), recognition as a person before the law (6), equality before the law without discrimination (6 and 7), a fair trial in any charge brought against a person (10), the presumption that an accused person is innocent until proved guilty (11), freedom of movement within a State and the right to leave it and return to it (13), the right to a nationality (15), the right to marry and found a family (16), the right to have private property (17), freedom of thought, conscience and religion, including the right to practise religion in private and in public (18), freedom of opinion and expression (19) and of peaceful assembly and association (20), the right to take part in government directly or through representatives (noting that 'the will of the people shall be the basis of the authority of government') (21), the right to social security (22), to work ('everyone has the right to equal pay for equal work') (23), to rest and leisure and holidays with pay (24), to an adequate standard of living (25), and to education ('parents have a prior right to choose the kind of education that shall be given to their children'—a clause that could easily nullify the intention of the article) (26).

How far are these pious platitudes? The American Declaration of Independence was the actual basis of an actual revolution and could be implemented in a political structure. This Declaration of Human Rights, already violated by most of the large nations, is not attached to any effective political instrument. Nevertheless although it cannot make people do right it can deprive them of all respectable reasons for doing wrong, and it remains not only a challenge to things as they are but also an inspiration for those who wish to change them.

Don Salvador de Madariaga makes a very penetrating comment on the question of 'human rights'. He says that the idea is too limited and too individual. What we need to discuss is not human rights but human relations. Everybody believes in these rights for himself—it is when they lay on him the obligation to concede them to others that the trouble begins. Moreover in the present world we live in groups, and every consideration of human rights must deal with man and his fellows in whatever association they happen to be found together.

In the official book from which are taken both the Declaration of Human Rights and Dr Madariaga's comment upon it[1] there are three essays of particular interest in the context of our present discussion. Professor Chung-Shu Lo writes on 'Human rights in the Chinese tradition'. (This was written before China became Communist.) Referring to an old Chinese classic, he says (in words almost the same as those of Dr Price's sermon at the Old Jewry in 1789) that 'when the ruler no longer rules for the welfare of the people it is the right of the people to revolt against him and dethrone him'. He also quotes from Mencius (372–289 B.C.): 'People are of primary importance. The State is of less importance. The sovereign is of least importance.' He goes on to say that 'the basic ethical concept of Chinese social and political relations is the fulfilment of the duty to one's neighbour rather than the claiming of rights'—thereby illustrating the point of view of Dr Madariaga.

A Moslem point of view is put by an Indian professor, Dr Humayum Kabir, in a very jejune statement of only four pages. He cannot refrain from trailing his coat. Thus he says: 'There is one fundamental flaw in the Western conception of human rights. Whatever be the theory, in practice they are often applied only to Europeans.' He then suggests four fundamental rights 'on the enjoyment of which all other rights depend'. These are the rights to food and clothing, to housing, to education and to medical attention. 'It will be noticed', he says, 'that they appertain to the security rather than the liberty of the individual. This is only a recognition of the fact that liberty is essentially a social concept and has no significance outside society.'

Mr S. V. Puntambekar of Nagpur presents 'The Hindu concept of human rights' in an equally short statement which, as we might expect, begins at the metaphysical end: 'Man has in him a deeper self, call it soul or spirit..., it is the nature of this man to

[1] *Human Rights: a Symposium edited by UNESCO* (Wingate, 1949).

search for the true, the good and the beautiful.' From this he passes to a consideration of the worldliness of men today, and says that therefore 'we shall have to give up some of the superstitions of material science and limited reason which make man too much this-worldly, and introduce higher spiritual aims and values for mankind'. There are five social freedoms—from violence, want, exploitation, dishonour, early death and disease—and these are matched by five virtues—tolerance, compassion, knowledge, freedom of conscience, and freedom from fear. These last five are there to control the first five, and human rights consist in the enjoyment of all ten, but he adds at the end: 'We in India also want freedom from foreign rule and civil warfare.'

These three statements are depressing, and they make one anxious about the future of the world, in which the Eastern countries and Islam are likely to play a greater and greater part. Western learning and particularly Western political ideas have given Eastern thought a framework which it seemed unable to produce for itself. This framework, however, in the West has had a foundation of Christian ethics and Roman law. How far it can be of use without such a foundation remains to be seen. It is one of the most vexing problems of our time. And at the root of all our frustrations, both in East and West, is the fact of original sin. It is the sinfulness of man that creates these problems, and of that fact no notice at all is taken in any of these statements on human rights.

## CHAPTER VIII

# LIBERTY

### I THE 'SECULAR TRINITY'

For the working out of the relations of Church and State in some detail I have taken the familiar slogan of the French revolutionaries —'liberty, equality and fraternity'. Although crimes have been committed in the names of every one of them they nevertheless represent permanent factors which have to be reckoned with in every society whether free or unfree. It has been doubted before now whether all three can exist together—whether liberty, for instance, can exist along with equality—and we may admit at once that there is a certain amount of overlapping as well as a certain amount of mutual antagonism. It is possible, however, to study them to some extent apart, and in our concern for the relations of Church and State we shall endeavour to do so. On the whole a consideration of liberty has to do mainly with the relation of the institution to the individual or the group, whether the institution is the Church or the State. The reference is also to the Church as one institution in relation to the State as another institution. Again, a discussion of equality brings up the question of the attitude of both Church and State to private property and also the acid question of the relation of liberty and equality. And the consideration of fraternity involves discussion of ideals and practice, and the measure of allowance which we are to make to persons as against principles in matters such as marriage and divorce and Christian unity. The question of the establishment of religion involves so many of these that it is being considered separately.

## 2 LIBERTY AN ETHICAL CONCEPT. J. S. MILL AND J. FITZJAMES STEPHEN

In 1933 the Nazis burnt down the Reichstag building in Berlin and they set the blame upon a Bulgarian Communist, Georgi Dimitrov. His fearless defence in court had such an effect on his enemies that it was difficult to believe that it was he and not they who stood in the dock. Indeed Göring loudly announced that he himself would attend the trial 'to show that he was not afraid of Dimitrov!' The accused gained his freedom and his story caused a thrill of admiration around the world.

Time went by. The war ended and in 1946 Dimitrov returned home from Russia to be Communist Prime Minister of Bulgaria. The next year he followed the Soviet model and all the opposition parties were liquidated. His crowning infamy was to put on 'trial' Nikola Petkov, the leader of the Agrarian party and one of the most heroic figures in Bulgarian democracy. Despite protests from all over the world including Britain and the United States Petkov was executed, hounded to death by the very man who in Berlin had made so notable a stand for freedom.

It is clear from this that liberty can find no firm foundation simply in the protest against power, because all too often it is a protest not against power as such but against power in the hands of other men. This may happen on the national scale, but it happens also daily in committee meetings of every kind. As Litvinov said of peace so we can say of liberty that it is one and indivisible.

Liberty from the Christian point of view means freedom of the spirit, that is to say primarily liberation from the dominion of sin and all those lower motives which beset mankind in its struggle after character. It is something that is not there at the beginning, it is the reward of effort and the gift of grace. It means freedom from fear, from the tyranny of moods, from frustration, indolence and boredom, from sin and from self. This is the primary freedom which is regulative of all others. If this goes wrong everything else goes wrong. All other freedoms that a man has are freedoms in relation to his fellows. This alone is an inner freedom the secret of which is in a man's own soul and from which all other freedoms proceed. The story of the Fall of Man is a Biblical myth but it represents a psychological fact of which most men are only too fully aware. It did not require Freud to convince us of the perpetual warfare that goes on both in and for the soul of man. St Paul noted it long ago in his letter to the Romans. There is no fact about human nature more radical than this. It is here that the best laid schemes of social reformers have gone adrift. It is here that many a character laden with promise has gone down in shame and sorrow. Dimitrov unfortunately represents one of the commonest types of human nature.

Liberty, therefore, has about it an ethical quality, for it is a positive condition of the person and a release from all hindrances to excellence. Far from being a mere absence of interference, it may actually require interference of a kind. T. H. Green's famous definition of freedom brings in all these factors.[1] Freedom, he said, is that condition of things in which, when a man is faced with two choices, he naturally and inevitably chooses the good. There must, of course, be a genuine choice. A man cannot be free unless he is free to choose. But being free to choose he is still not free if he chooses evil, for in that case he is enslaved by his lower nature. If it be said for the sake of argument that if he chooses good he is being equally enslaved by his *higher* nature, that is precisely what it does mean. Paul, the bondslave of Christ, rejoiced in the freedom with which Christ had made him free. This may sound like a paradox but it is an inevitable result of the conditions of our life here on earth. We are social beings and our liberty has to be equated with the liberty of other people. We are also moral beings and our liberty depends on our choice between good and evil or between good and better. The author of the book of Deuteronomy puts it in an epigram, 'See, I have set before thee this day life and good, and death and evil,...therefore choose life.'

This ethical factor enters into all situations where liberty is involved. It is regulative of all others and without it there can be no true liberty. But men often fight for sectional aims—political

[1] In *Principles of Political Obligation.*

liberty, economic liberty, religious liberty, and even for more specific aims within these sections—such as vote by ballot as the way to political liberty, nationalization as the way to economic liberty, disestablishment as the way to religious liberty—and thereby they come into fierce antagonism with their fellows. Liberty cannot be defined in sectional terms: it must take into account the whole state of man. Some men have fought for liberty of a kind and have achieved it, but in the gaining of it they have lost their own souls. Dimitrov is an example of such.

Just as the whole state of man has to be considered, so also has the whole community of mankind. No man can be truly free while his brother is a slave. 'In giving freedom to the slave', said Abraham Lincoln in his message to Congress on 1 December 1862, 'we assure freedom to the free.' There is a solidarity of the human race which makes inevitable this application of the principle that liberty is indivisible. If victory by itself is an impermanent type of human relationship so too is liberty when it is conceived in sectional, national, class, and racial terms. It is not only the blacks who are enslaved in South Africa, it is the whites also, even those in the government. And so too are we in Britain and mankind everywhere. There can be no contracting out of the human community. Where one suffers all suffer with him and where one rejoices then all rejoice. Here is the fundamental error into which democratic communities and churches are continually falling. They imagine that spiritual qualities can be localized, that one place can enjoy them while another goes short, that one church can hold the truth and all others are in error. The very assumption itself is an indication of the activity of its opposite.

Much of this kind of erroneous argument arises because liberty is conceived in abstract terms. It is thought out in the study and then applied or misapplied to an actual situation. Consequently liberty is equated with non-interference by the Government, as the Liberal industrialists conceived of it in the nineteenth century, or it is supposed to be assured by freedom of contract between employer and worker, or it is assumed to be sufficient that the expression of opinion should be free. These have the appearance of concreteness, but in reality they are corollaries from an abstract idea of liberty. It was this that inspired Sir James Fitzjames Stephen's attack on John Stuart Mill's book *On Liberty*. Mill's book was published in 1859 and it has been one of the most influential books in the world's history. Nevertheless its basic assumption, that if liberty is to exist government must keep its hands off, is a pure abstraction which in practice could be used to permit the worst excesses of capitalism. That, of course, was not what Mill intended, but this static conception of liberty could not but have that result. Sir James Fitzjames Stephen during his sojourn in India in 1869–72 noticed that steps were there being taken towards the achievement of liberty not by diminishing government interference but by increasing it. His book *Liberty, Equality, Fraternity* was based on this experience. Once we give up the idea of liberty as an assertion of rights, the true function of government begins to appear. It exists for the maintenance of society rather than for a balancing of claims. Stephen found that British rule in India, acting in the name of liberty, had interfered at five important points in the life of that country. It had forced upon the people, against the will of many of them, the principle that people of different religions must live at peace with one another, and that change of religion must not involve civil disabilities. (This cut at the root of Brahminism.) It had set up a system of education alien to the principles of Hinduism and Islam, and it had forbidden such Indian religious rites as *suttee*, the immolation of widows on the death of their husbands. Lastly, it had given members of an alien faith freedom to preach their gospel without disturbance.

It will be noticed that every one of these five points illustrates what might be called an enforcement of freedom. It means ensuring freedom to one group by limiting that of others. If we look at the progress of individual liberty in Britain in the last hundred years we shall see precisely the same process at work—the liberating of one class of the community by checking the liberty of another class. The apparent arbitrariness of this proceeding can be justified only if we look on liberty as an ethical condition. To take away a man's liberty to do mischief, to take away his power to tyrannize over other people, is not taking away his liberty in its widest sense: it is making possible his liberty as well as theirs. The whole idea of 'interference' would be an anachronism in a free society. 'That which touches all shall be approved of all' is an old political maxim dating from the thirteenth century and where there is government of the people, for the people and by the people 'interference' is not the correct term to use.

Mill's position has, however, been taken up by all kinds of people with sectional aims. Emil Brunner, for instance, in his book *Justice and the Social Order* divides his subject into two parts, first, principles, and second, practice—as if the working of human relationships could first of all be thought out in solitude and then brought down into the market place and applied to the varied throbbing life of the world. Perhaps theologians are even more prone to this kind of sectional attitude than any other people. In one of the latest books on our theme, *Christianity and Economic Problems*, the author, D. L. Munby of Aberdeen University, shows the weakness of this kind of approach as we find it in Canon Demant's *Theology of Society* and his *Religion and the Decline of Capitalism*. The theologians seem nearly always to begin at the metaphysical end, as far as possible away from the people whom they are supposed to be talking about and hence there is an inevitable dissociation in what is called the 'application' of religion to human life. In this, however, they are not alone. They are in a mixed bag with philosophers like Hobbes, who argued from a mythical social contract, and reformers like Rousseau, who argued from an equally mythical 'general will', and ideologists like Karl Marx and Engels, who argued from an ideal society where all surplus value went to labour, where there were no classes and no State and where a purely hypothetical body, the proletariat, would have everything all its own way.

This criticism applies not only to liberty but also to equality and fraternity and every other aspect of human relationships. It might be well, therefore, to clear up this matter before going any further. Where are these principles of liberty to come from if not from men's thinking? If men have no idea what they want to achieve, how can they persuade other people to join them in achieving it? The answer lies in the fact that not all the relevant factors are in sight at the beginning. They come into view as one goes along. Suppose the early Christians had attempted to work out the principles of an ideal Christian society, what would have been its characteristics? It would almost certainly have accepted slavery as an inevitable factor in social structure. It would certainly have included community of goods. What it could not have included would have been the internationalizing of industry and commerce, universal suffrage, sex equality, and all the manifold discoveries of science which have altered the complexion of the world. How have these later developments come to have a moral and even a religious tinge? How is it that slavery, war and capitalism are all nowadays religious questions coming under the judgement of Christ as they could not have been in the first century? Only by men using the light that they had and so receiving more light. This seems to me to be characteristic of the Christian Gospel as against every other religion of mankind. More and more is revealed as you go along and at every stage dogmatic theology has to be rewritten in the light of new revelation. Is not this contained in the saying of Christ to his disciples, 'He that believeth on me...greater works than these shall he do; because I go to my Father'?

Is not this principle true also of the growth of liberty and the development of law, at any rate in England? The remark of Sir Henry Sumner Maine which we have already quoted is relevant to a number of situations besides the one he had in mind.[1] By saying that in England 'substantive law is secreted in the interstices of procedure' he meant that a body of principles is not something with which you start but something that is the result of taking events as they come and treating them in accordance with the best light you have at the time. In Scriptural terms it is by doing the will that you come to know the doctrine.[2] In philosophical terms it is the Aristotelian approach rather than the

[1] Above, p. 45.

[2] John vii. 17.

Platonic. And it is justified because the material you are dealing with is living human beings and not abstract ideas. Accordingly, a static view of liberty cannot be permanent, and to begin with a blue-print of the ideal society means adapting human beings to fit in with your pattern; it is to subordinate persons to theories and it assumes that the whole truth, present and future, is in your possession *now*. This, of course, was the calm assumption of the medieval Church, of the Calvinists in Geneva and of Communists everywhere. Calvin's theory of society was a deduction from his metaphysical idea of the nature of God. When it came to be applied to human beings it could make sense only on the assumption of the total depravity of mankind. The State therefore must have coercive power to keep in check the waywardness of the human family. Karl Marx began with a theory of the classless society as an ideal. In practice it has worked out to the elimination of everybody whose views are not the same as the government's, and of course the assumption is that Big Brother knows best. But the only way in which society can be organized along Christian lines is as a family of friends, linked together in free association by a common loyalty.

## 3 DELEGATES OR REPRESENTATIVES?

In their conception of political liberty our forefathers held that no one should have the vote except those who had a 'stake in the country'. This was interpreted always as property, and the justification of the position was that the propertied classes could have no interest in violent change and were therefore a steadying force in the body politic. They had a stake in the country. Parliament, a limited electorate, government, property and coercion were all on one side, and on the other was the great majority of the population. It was natural, therefore, for the unfranchised to interpret liberty in terms of the franchise, and to hold that voting power was equivalent to liberty.

Today the franchise has been extended almost as far as it can go, for in a free society *everybody* has a stake in the country. Property is no longer the standard. The assets of a country are not its land or its property but its free people. It is an interesting comment on the present position that the trade unions are gradually beginning to accept this fact. Mr John Boyd, a recent candidate for the secretaryship of the Amalgamated Engineering Union of Britain, said to his people on the eve of a threatened strike:

> Never in history have the workers of this country been so country-conscious. They know that if the economy of this country breaks down, they break down with it. A week's stoppage would do irreparable damage to the country. We no longer represent a hungry mob crying out for bread. We represent people earning a reasonable standard of living, and they are not prepared to throw that away.[1]

These are very important words, for they indicate a change in trade union attitudes that was bound to come. The unions came into existence partly as friendly societies, often indeed with religious ideals,[2] to provide fellowship for their members and to look after them in sickness and ill health but still more to fight for higher wages, shorter hours and improved conditions. While Parliament was the preserve of the few and those few with the stake in the country (old style) the only weapon that the trade unions could use was that of the strike. The strike was against the employers, and Parliament in the first instance did not come in at all. But now with working men not only having the vote but also controlling a large section of Parliament itself the strike weapon is out of date. It is interesting therefore that, while Parliament is becoming more and more concerned with economic questions and economic procedures, the trade unions have the opportunity to become more and more politically minded and to turn towards political action. Unfortunately the organization of the unions themselves is proving very much out of date in present circumstances. In an increasing number of industries it is the shop stewards of the individual factories that have the effective power. Power here as everywhere else has a corrupting influence and it is seen in the proneness of shop stewards constantly to seek a trial

[1] Reported in the *Manchester Guardian* and the *Daily Telegraph* and given a headline in the *News Chronicle*, but not reported in *The Times*; 9 January 1957.

[2] Below, p. 94.

of strength with the employers. A disconcertingly large number of strikes in British industries since the war have been due to no other cause than this.

With Parliament at hand for the discussion of disputes the use of the strike becomes much more clearly a strike against the whole community even more than against individual employers. Some time ago, during a bus strike in London, *Punch* came out with a sardonic cartoon. It showed a little group of people on a wet night huddled together under a lamp-post and waiting for the bus that would never come. The caption was the demand familiar in labour disputes, 'No victimization!' This put in a nutshell the situation. One section of the community had victimized another section but did not themselves wish to be victimized. Nothing could illustrate better the nature of an inorganic society. Liberty cannot really be won at the cost of someone else's victimization.

A further corollary follows from the recognition of Parliament as the expression of society rather than of a governing class. The extension of parliamentary responsibility over health, employment, pensions, marketing, food, education, raw materials and every other aspect of human life necessarily involves a vast increase in bureaucracy. Public services do not run themselves. Bureaucracy is a word that has come to have a bad meaning, but in so far as it is a vital occupation there is no reason for this. The bureaucrat, however, suffers obloquy on two counts—when he has too much initiative and when he has none at all. A bureaucrat of the first type enjoys the use of his power both over his colleagues and over those whom he assumes to be subject to him. From this sort of man the ordinary citizen is likely to find his liberty endangered as we have already seen in the case of Crichel Down.[1] The second type stands by the letter of the law, is unaware of mitigating circumstances, works constantly to rule, lives in fear of rebuke from the man above him. I remember one such who, when the war broke out and he was responsible for evacuating the children from his area to another part of the country, took to his bed and remained there until the operation was successfully

[1] Above, p. 36.

carried out by his deputy, who had no scruples at all about using initiative. Such men clog the wheels of industry by steadily getting in the way of the technician's or the manager's legitimate use of discretion. Incentive in industry is killed at various levels and by different causes in the welfare state, but at the managerial level to kill incentive is to kill industry itself and so some of our ablest technicians are emigrating to countries where they believe they will have a freer hand.

It is here where Parliament, representing the country as a whole, may vindicate liberty against a high-handed administrator. The Crichel Down case was only one of many. This is an unexpected reversal of its earlier role in which Parliament itself on occasion provided a threat to individual liberty.

The constitution of Parliament itself raises a further question of liberty, which has become increasingly important with the arrival of Labour governments. So far we have been concerned with the freedom of the worker and the freedom of the ordinary citizen. But what of the freedom of members of Parliament themselves? Is the member a representative or is he a delegate? Is he, that is to say, free to exercise his own judgement as questions arise or is he there simply to register the opinions of the constituency that put him in? The answer is complicated by the fact that while he stands for a territorial unit his expenses may have been paid by people outside the constituency altogether. To whom then does he owe obedience—to his constituency or to the people who have provided the financial and other support?

The classic case that raises this issue was Burke's famous speech to the electors of Bristol in 1773. He was one of two members elected in that year, and his colleague had declared that he would put himself entirely at the disposal of his constituents. Burke spoke in disagreement. Speaking of the function of a parliamentary representative, he said:

> ...his unbiased opinion, his mature judgement, his enlightened conscience he ought not to sacrifice to you, to any man or to any set of men living. Your representative owes you not his industry only, but his judgement; and he betrays instead of serving you if he sacrifices it

to your opinion.... Government and legislation are matters of reason and judgement and not of inclination: and what sort of reason is that in which the determination precedes the discussion, in which one set of men deliberate and another decide, and where those who form the conclusion are perhaps three hundred miles distant from those who hear the arguments?[1]

This issue is a very serious one at the present moment both in England and in America. In England the issue arises in both central and local government. A man is elected to Parliament by a majority vote. Two questions then arise. First, whom does he represent in the constituency—the people who put him in or everybody? Philip Snowden's answer was that once a man is elected he represents the entire constituency and not his party only. Accordingly, Snowden used to sit in his office in Accrington every Saturday morning to be consulted by any of his constituents no matter to what party they belonged. This is surely the proper attitude, otherwise at every election the losing party is simply disfranchised.

But the second question is even more serious. What is to be his attitude to the party Whip? Is he expected to vote as he is told, and

...to leave his brains outside
And vote just as his leaders tell him to

or is he free to use his own judgement? Over the question of the Suez Canal some Conservative as well as some Labour members voted against their party and were duly rebuked. Some years earlier on the eve of the Italian elections in 1947 a number of British members of Parliament exercised their free judgement by sending their greetings to one of the contending parties and were very severely censured by their own party leaders. By what right do the party chiefs take action such as this? Is it assumed that elected members of Parliament cease to be free men by reason of their new position, and that they are delegates rather than representatives? Conservatives as a rule are more independent of the party machine but a further issue arises in their case. When one notices the large number of business directorships that are held by

[1] *Burke*, by John Morley, p. 75; Erskine May, *Constitutional History of England*, II, pp. 70–1.

some Conservatives the question might well be asked whether they represent their constituents or their business interests.

Taking everything into account, however, the territorial unit is a sound basis of representation, if for no other reason than that the member represents both those who voted for him and those who voted against. There is a certain astringent element in this situation which is good for both sides. If a member can keep his constituents with him he is less at the mercy of outside interests, while they may on occasion find it more important to vote for the man rather than for the party. Burke spoke once of what he called the cant of 'not men, but measures' which he said was 'a sort of charm by which many people get loose from every honourable engagement'.

In local government similar questions crop up. In some areas, indeed, the hold of the party machine over the members is far more rigid than in the case of Parliament and defeats any attempt at government on democratic lines. When a council meeting is due each party caucus meets beforehand and, before they can hear any arguments from the other side, make up their minds how they are going to vote. The determination does more than precede the discussion: it takes the place of it. The official meetings themselves are often quite farcical for that very reason.

In America the legislators often suffer almost beyond endurance from 'pressure groups' of every sort. Various interests, industrial, commercial, ecclesiastical, and a dozen more, keep their representatives in Washington and these are hard on the heels of Congressmen when any relevant issue arises. There is also a good deal of 'legislation by newspapers', and legislators are apt to be more concerned about newspaper men than about the constituents whom they are supposed to represent. How can men vindicate freedom when they themselves are not free? The fear that has been struck into the heart of every public man by the bizarre operations of various committees appointed to smell out Communism makes men more violent in speech and action than they would otherwise be and makes sober judgement not only difficult but often even dangerous.

## 4 FROM CONTRACT TO STATUS

Political liberty was the aim of the Liberal party in Britain in the nineteenth century, and it was conceived in terms of the ballot and the franchise. With the typically British fondness for political rather than revolutionary action the working men's representatives in Parliament and in the trade unions attached themselves to the Liberal party. In the world of industry Liberal principles, derived from John Stuart Mill, meant freedom of contract. Under the system of *laissez-faire* it was believed that employers and employed should be brought together on a basis of legal contract which was enforceable on both sides. This would give security to the working man who was the chief sufferer in the earlier unorganized system.

It was discovered, however, that liberty of contract was liberty only in name. It was a political device to remedy an economic evil. It looked democratic but it was at bottom the very opposite. It meant that the employers were free to decide the terms on which they would offer work, and the men were free to take it or leave it. If they took it the position was stabilized at that point and any alteration on either side was a breach of contract. If they refused it they were free to starve. All the cards were in the employers' hands. The only effective remedy, and even that was not very effective, was to go on strike. Striking was an inevitable accompaniment of freedom of contract as it was then understood. It was part of the system of conflicting claims on which industry was organized, and, as we have seen, liberty in the full sense cannot be achieved by such a system.

Keir Hardie, the Scottish miners' leader, shared the general disillusionment, and saw that without a wider extension of the idea of liberty than the Liberals were prepared to grant there was no economic future for the working man on a basis of contract. Accordingly, in 1888 he cut loose from the Liberals and founded the Independent Labour Party. It is interesting, and again characteristic of the British, that the 'independence' of the I.L.P. was not meant to be independence of Parliament, for it accepted political methods, but from now onwards the political machine would be worked by the labouring classes themselves instead of having the Liberals to work it for them.

A general movement was at work in the country along the same lines as those indicated by the Labour revolt, a movement away from contract and in the direction of status. Contract is concerned only with labour: status is concerned with the labourer as well. The failure of freedom of contract as a satisfactory basis for industry arose from the fact that instead of a personal relationship it substituted what was called the 'cash nexus', and labour became a commodity to be bought and sold in the self-regulating market just like any other commodity. This is what was meant by 'capitalism' in its nineteenth-century form. The employer bought labour and as long as he got it he was under no obligation to himself or to the community to care anything at all about the labourer. It was this which so angered Karl Marx. He saw it as a case of power versus weakness and he would have remedied it by turning the system upside down with the dictation of the proletariat in place of that of the capitalist. His diagnosis was correct, but his suggested remedy was no remedy at all, for it did not go to the root of the trouble. The situation had in it far more than power versus weakness. It was a case of an altogether inorganic, mechanical view of society as a cluster of warring atoms instead of a human family in which differences did not become disabilities. In other words contract was a merely mechanical device for dealing with a human situation and therefore it failed. There can never be peace on earth nor will men ever be truly free until they are recognized as persons and themselves recognize other people as the same—all members of the one human family.

As we have already noticed,[1] it was on the basis of status that the medieval Church State was organized, but status under feudalism meant a static society. Except through the Church, and later on through the towns, there was no hope of anybody rising out of the class into which he had been born. God had created them high and lowly and ordered their estate and there was nothing therefore that could be done about it. The system of

[1] Above, p. 51.

feudalism died in England centuries ago, but the attitude associated with it has long persisted. It was still there in the days of the Industrial Revolution and it prevented the Church of that age from taking a realistic, let alone a Christian, view of the situation. The old terminology such as 'master' and 'apprentice' was allowed to dominate the situation long after the reality of it had gone. For instance, the pauper children who were sent up by wagon loads from London to mills in the North were still called 'apprentices' although there was no craft or skill whatever for them to learn.[1] Interference by government through the mildest of Factory Acts (1802) was condemned as breaking up the beautiful paternal relationship of master and apprentice! Consequently it was not surprising that the reformers sought to change this bogus relationship into an individual legal contract. Freedom of contract was looked upon as a great step in advance, as indeed at that time it undoubtedly was.

But status in the modern sense is not the same as status in the medieval sense. It is not a static unchangeable arrangement with a divine sanction backed up by the secular power. It is a recognition that a man is a man and not a work-producing machine, that he is part of a complex of interests—family, community, church, club, and so forth—that what society owes to him is the circumstances in which he can give the best of which he is capable and can receive what he requires in order to do so. Therefore we have family allowances, holidays with pay, sick benefit, unemployment insurance, medical attendance, pensions, and all the other apparatus of the welfare state. The old type of employer and capitalist is dying out. He is being replaced by the manager and the technician. More and more our countrymen are becoming dependent on salaries and less and less on unearned income. Labour is ceasing to be a commodity, and both management and workers are gaining the status of—to use a much abused term—civil servants. As society becomes more and more free industry becomes a service—a service in which is freedom. Naturally this is not happening all at once, and while on the whole management

[1] J. L. and B. Hammond, *The Rise of Modern Industry* (1937), p. 199.

has seen it before labour there is a great deal of talk and even action on both sides which assumes the continuance of an earlier state of things. A hundred and fifty years of opposition between labour and capital bred habits which are hard to break, and even able people like Aneurin Bevan use the old language and appear to accept the old assumptions. The transitional period is one of strife and misunderstanding but the set of affairs is in a healthier direction.

Here, however, a note of warning is needed. Part of the Communist case is precisely that which we have indicated—the need for human beings to be recognized as persons rather than as one part of the industrial machine. But Communism, while seeking to make a workman free of an employer, has no intention of allowing him to be free of its own ideology. It is rather like the attitude of the woman who took her unwilling little boy to the Zoo and said to him: 'I've brought you here to enjoy yourself and I'll clout you if you don't!' We shall look at this issue again when we come to consider 'fraternity'.

## 5 PRIVATE VICES, PUBLIC VIRTUES

'Man versus the State' has been a perpetual problem all down the ages. Herbert Spencer's solution, in his book with that title, was to sacrifice the State to the individual. Communists and others who have drunk at the Hegelian spring would sacrifice the individual to the State. It should be recognized, however, that apart from possession of the instruments of coercion (which raises another problem) the relation of man to the State (i.e. the Government) is but a special case of the relation of the individual to any institution whatever. As we are concerned here with the religious side of these questions we might begin by seeing what the Bible has to say on the subject.

'The sabbath was made for man, and not man for the sabbath.' This is far from being an isolated saying of Jesus. It represented in epigrammatic form his general attitude to this question. In order to get the full flavour of this saying we must put it into its context. The Sabbath was to the Jews an ordinance of God. It was one of the marks that distinguished Israel from the rest of the world. Its origin had been traced back to the beginning when God created the world. It had come to be surrounded by all kinds of regulations and taboos. There was no more sacred institution than this. Yet Jesus treats it with what must have seemed to his contemporaries a cavalier unconcern. The Sabbath is not an end in itself. It is not even primarily for the glory of God. It was made for man. We may ask ourselves what other institutions are 'made for man'—the Church, for instance, or the Eucharist, or marriage?

It is here that the clash comes between the Church as an institution and the Church invisible, between the ideal State and the actual State. In the eyes of the ideal Church one of the highest names given to the head of the Roman hierarchy is *Servus Servorum Dei*, the servant of the servants of God. But in actual practice this has to be equated with the magnificence of St Peter's, the Swiss Guards and the *ex cathedra* utterances of the popes on social and other questions. Similarly, on the secular side, we have to harmonize the rolling periods of the American Declaration of Independence, concerned to vindicate the rights of man to life, liberty and the pursuit of happiness, with the flat denial of some of these to some men because of their colour. In South Africa there are no heroes of the past so much honoured as the Voortrekkers who for the sake of freedom crossed the Vaal River to escape from British domination. It is clear, however, from the testimony of several of them that they took their slaves with them and that here lay the real motive of the Trek. The patient scholarship of Professor Eric Walker has shown how completely one-sided was the Voortrekkers' attachment to freedom.[1]

Membership of an institution, whether a church or a party or an organized group of any kind, has a very mixed effect on the human mind. It gives a man a representative character so that he is not just an individual, but the whole institution as it were coheres in him, and he gladly accepts that responsibility. He

[1] In *A History of South Africa* and *The Great Trek*.

acquires, so to speak, an extension of his personality. On the other hand a sharp contrast often appears between his private views and his public position. Bernard Mandeville's famous satire *The Fable of the Bees* (1714) has as its sub-title 'Private vices public virtues'. Men as members of a public institution will condone all manner of sharp practices which they would never condone in their private relationships. The institution is a screen behind which the most primitive instincts not only have free play but can be defended as working to the glory of God and the relief of man's estate. This is not to accuse anyone of dishonesty. The difference may indeed be due to a very proper regard for a sense of trusteeship in the institution, which can work either for or against the good of mankind. Nevertheless to ensure that it works for good rather than for evil needs a strong dose of disinfectant against egoism.

It is this deceptive regard for the institution that makes possible a justification of persecution both for religion and for politics. Let us hear Father Ronald Knox on the subject: 'You cannot bind over the Catholic Church, as the price of your adhesion to her doctrines, to waive all right of invoking the secular arm in defence of her own principles.'[1] This, of course, is a justification that would be seized upon by the Inquisition. Whereas it was true that the Protestants of Elizabeth I's day persecuted and burnt the Catholics when they got the chance, such persecution was flatly against Protestant principles and in the course of time has been seen to be so, but it is still an integral part of the Catholic position, as Father Knox's remark would indicate.

In our time we have seen a particularly vicious use of force on behalf of the institution in the Communist states. In an earlier century, rulers like James I would seek to make their opponents conform or, as he said, 'would harry them out of the land'. This our latter-day tyrants would look upon as a confession of failure on the part of the ruler. Accordingly nowadays instead of opponents of the regime being exiled they are deliberately prevented from leaving, and are either made the victims of sadistic cruelty or are subjected to such measures as 'brain washing' in

[1] *The Belief of Catholics* (1927), p. 241.

the attempt to remake their characters according to those of their persecutors.

Persecution, however, can exist at many levels. It is, for instance, a perpetual scandal in the eyes of some good people that cinemas should be open on Sundays and that football matches should also be played on Sundays. The Lord's Day Observance Society may not look on itself as a persecuting body but its use of the common informer procedure and the invocation of obsolete statutes to penalize if not to prevent such Sunday activities can hardly be called brotherly kindness. Methodists certainly do not consider themselves as persecutors, but there was warm applause at the action of a Methodist farmer, a lay preacher and a teetotaller, who bought up a village public house in order to close it, thus compelling the villagers to walk an extra six miles in order to quench their thirst. The 'monkey trial' in Tennessee was an attempt on the part of religious people to use the courts to prevent a teacher of biology who 'believed in evolution' (whatever that phrase may mean) from continuing to teach the young. The chief figure in this particular circus was William Jennings Bryan, who took the line that it was the function of the State to see that no views that 'contradicted the Bible' should be taught in the public schools. An individual may quite well believe that his own views are his own and that he has no right to force them upon other people who do not want them, but if those are the views of an institution to which he belongs, the desire to vindicate them and to have them universally accepted becomes in some cases almost pathological. There is in all of us a certain irritation when people disagree with us and apparently will not listen to reason, and the itch to force them to do so is often too strong to be resisted, especially if the instruments of coercion are readily at hand. To use power of any sort is a dangerous proceeding even when by consent of a majority. It may not actually corrupt, but even with the best of motives it warps judgement, creates a spiritually dangerous sense of superiority, and lowers the level of intention. We have seen the dire results of this attitude in the attempt to enforce prohibition of alcoholic drinks in America. But history is full of examples.

## 6 VOLUNTARY SOCIETIES

The Church in most Protestant countries is nowadays a voluntary society and like all such is feeling the consequences of the heavy taxation of its people. As more and more activities are taken over by the State and have to be paid for out of the taxes, the future of voluntary societies becomes increasingly difficult to foresee. Not only is money difficult to raise, but also the scope of a voluntary society is often reduced. Yet voluntary societies are a vital part of the life of a community. As the State by reason of its equation with society is becoming more and more omnicompetent there is all the more need for as many openings as possible for private initiative, unofficial authority and the opportunity to lead as well as to be led. There are people who have a touching belief in the effectiveness of State action in every department of life. The most fruitful approach to the problem, however, is by looking upon it not as a tug-of-war between government and private persons but rather as a sober assessment of what matters are most suitably and effectively carried out by public ownership and what are best left to private enterprise. The solution of this is not a matter of principle so much as of expediency. Neither private enterprise nor state control is sacrosanct.

Yet when we have made the decision there still remains the question whether the voluntary society can afford to carry out its obligations unassisted by grants. This has recently been a very acid problem in England with regard to the old grammar schools, some of them 'public schools'.[1] When there seemed no choice except between coming entirely under the State in the form of the Local Education Authority or raising endowments and fees, very many schools went 'all out for independence'. They may have been right, but the issue should have been faced on other grounds,

[1] In England a public school is one which is a member of the Headmasters' Conference, has a large sixth form (i.e. ages 16–18), has a considerable number of old pupils at the universities, and is free from control by statutory bodies such as the Local Education Authority. It is 'public' because its profits are ploughed back into the school, as against private or proprietary schools whose profits go to the private owners and as against State or 'County' schools which charge no fees, and so have no profits at all.

namely whether the children would be better off or less well off if the school came under the Authority. Some schools that have done so have not been materially changed from what they were before. Headmasters' and headmistresses' reports on Speech Days have given very little token of the change of status. There are, however, some Education Authorities whose temper would justify any school struggling with all its might to keep its independence.

The independence of schools is a separate question from that of grants. The Roman Catholics raise a very special issue on this point. It is not always realized how much the use of teaching orders of monks and nuns in Roman Catholic schools is a financial benefit to the Church itself. These people receive no salary and yet in England Local Authority grants are payable to them on the Burnham Scale. Such payments make no difference at all to the individuals, but save the Church authorities a good deal of expense and are subsidies for the institution. This practice works to an even greater extent in the mission field, where Protestant missions are at a considerable disadvantage compared with the Catholics. In the eyes of the more prejudiced Protestants Bernard Manderville's quip is reversed, and private virtues become public vices.

## 7 THE FREEDOM OF THE INSTITUTION. REVISED PRAYER BOOK OF 1928. THE SCOTTISH CHURCHES' CASE

The relation of the individual to the institution, whether it be Church or State, raises the further question of the freedom of the institution itself, whether in Church or State and whether local or national, official or voluntary.

J. N. Figgis in his book *Churches in the Modern State* describes how individual liberty came about in England.

> In the seventeenth century it was not the isolated individual but the religious body, the sect, with its passionate assertion of its own right to be, which finally won toleration from the State. By himself, apart from religious discord, the individual would have secured no freedom. It was the competing claims of religious bodies, the inability of any single one

to destroy the others, which finally secured liberty. The rights of man was their recognition of the sense of his duties towards God. Political liberty is the fruit of ecclesiastical animosities.[1]

This is a cheerful conclusion, and yet it was not the final conclusion, for the principle was capable of infinite extension. The individual has had to vindicate his own liberty against the sect itself, and it is this which has displayed, according to Dean Inge, the 'fissiparous nature of Protestantism'.

Figgis's reminder, however, is timely in two ways. First of all, the mainspring of the struggle for liberty has been religious zeal, and secondly, men have fought not for themselves alone but for themselves as part of a group. All that has been said about the value of the group as an extension of a man's own personality and experience is illustrated by the vigour with which men fight for causes. There is a vicariousness about it also, which itself is a religious principle, for men will fight for aims which can never be realized in their own lifetime, knowing, in Pauline language, that the sufferings of the present time are not to be compared with the glory that shall be revealed hereafter. Sidney Webb in his short history of the Durham miners points out that in the early days the great impetus towards trade unionism came from the Primitive Methodists. Nearly all the trade union leaders belonged to this body and their struggle for liberty against the coal-owners was an expression of their religious experience. In those early days while the religious principle of liberty was their mainstay their specific bargaining weapon was that they did good work which was not, but ought to be, recognized. Today when freedom has been gained and the present generation are enjoying what their forefathers themselves could never enjoy there is far less sense of obligation to do good work. Liberty again is one and indivisible and the man who is the victim of indolence cannot be said to be free. It is at this point that the Church needs to come in, for the freedom of the welfare state makes it harder, not easier, to achieve that inner freedom of the spirit.

The struggle of the groups for freedom has had another side to

[1] *Churches in the Modern State* (1914), p. 101.

it besides securing freedom for the individual and freedom of association for the members of the group. There has been the very acute problem of the freedom of the group to be what it wishes to be. In other words there is the question of the group's right to determine the law of its own being without interference from outside.

The illustrations of this are nearly all concerned with churches, for it is of the essence of a Christian church that it should be free to follow the guidance of the Spirit. A ready example of the need for this freedom was the defeat in 1928 of the Revised Prayer Book of the Church of England. The revision was the product of some years of thoughtful preparation and it was believed to have brought the book more into line with modern Anglican opinion. The Church of England being the established Church of the nation and thereby in a peculiar relation to the Government had to present the book for approval to Parliament. Parliament rejected it, and when it was submitted again with certain emendations it was rejected again. I shall have something to say later about the principle of establishment, but here we have to notice that Parliament, headed by a Prime Minister who was a Welsh Baptist, denied the right to a corporate body to make rules for itself which were not intended to be effective outside its own borders. The Church of England like every living body inevitably changes with the changing times, and to bind it without hope of change to a liturgy drawn up over three centuries ago was a denial of liberty. The situation no doubt was complicated by the fact that the Church is an established Church and therefore it can be argued that Parliament as representing the entire nation was the right body to decide the limits to which the nation's Church should be allowed to go, but this does not alter the fact that here was an institution deprived of the liberty to decide its own rules.

The classic case, however, in this regard is the Scottish Churches' case of 1904.

On 31 October 1900, the Free Church of Scotland united with the United Presbyterian Church to form the United Free Church of Scotland. A small dissenting minority of the Free Church served a summons on all the trustees of the former Free Church and also upon all the members of the Union Assembly on the ground that, by uniting with the United Presbyterians, a body with certain tenets different from its own, the Free Church (so it was argued) had departed from both the doctrinal and the legal standards of its constitution. The property, therefore, of the Free Church should of right belong only to those who had kept strictly to the old faith of the fathers of the Disruption in 1843 when the Free Church was founded. They desired the courts to pronounce that they alone were the historic Free Church. They were unsuccessful in the Scottish courts but, in August 1904, the House of Lords on appeal and by a majority decision gave judgement in their favour. By this judgement the whole of the property of the Free Church—churches, manses, colleges, everything which had been maintained by 1700 ministers and half a million Church members—passed into the possession of a little group of thirty ministers, nearly all of them in the remote Highlands. The judgement was so shocking that a Royal Commission had to be appointed which divided the property more in accordance with the real situation and this was made legal by an Act of Parliament.[1]

This is a case which raises the fundamental principle of the liberty of a group to reorganize itself from within, and it is not complicated like the Prayer Book controversy by the fact or establishment. The United Free Church was a voluntary society, in its polity entirely free from state control.

The law lords who tried the case were seven, of whom two, Lords Macnaghten and Lindley, dissented from the decision. Among the counsel for the United Free Church was Mr R. B. Haldane, afterwards Lord Haldane, whose task it was, in the somewhat cynical words of J. N. Figgis, 'to place the result of his meditations on the true meaning of the Westminster Confession before the characteristically Anglo-Saxon mentality of Lord Halsbury and Lord James of Hereford'.[2] The whole situation was quite incongruous and extremely humiliating. But it did bring

[1] P. Carnegie Simpson, *Life of Principal Rainy*, II, chapter 25.
[2] *Churches in the Modern State* (1914), p. 34.

to light certain principles of group structure which merit further notice. The first quotation is from Haldane's opening speech:

> The Church is like an organism; the materials may change, and there may be metabolism of every item of which it consists, and yet the Church goes on preserving its organic life through the medium of its system of Church government which provides for a supreme assembly, supreme in that matter of doctrine to which your Lordship referred and which I agree was a distinctive matter of doctrine at the time the Church was founded.[1]

The second passage comes from Lord Macnaghten's judgement:

> The question therefore seems to me to be this: Was the Church thus purified—the Free Church—so bound and tied by the tenets of the Church of Scotland prevailing at the time of Disruption, that departure from those tenets in any matter of substance would be a violation of that profession or testimony which may be called *the unwritten charter* of her foundation, and so necessarily involve a breach of trust in the administration of funds contributed for no other purpose but the support of the Free Church—the Church of the Disruption? Was the Free Church by the very condition of her existence forced to cling to her Subordinate Standards with so desperate a grip that she has lost hold and touch of the Supreme Standard of her faith? Was she from birth incapable of all growth and development? Was she (in a word) a dead branch and not a living Church? This, I think, is the real and only question.[2]

Lord Macnaghten was surely right in this judgement. For an institution to be held in mortmain when its founder dies is surely no honour to the founder. Liberty here is connected with the idea of continuity. One conception of continuity requires strict adherence to the system and ideas of the past in the form in which they have come down to us. The other is a continuity of spirit which is the same all down the ages although the form may change. I am credibly informed that all the materials of my body change every seven years. If this be true I am nevertheless aware that I am the same person who went to a certain school half a century ago. My identity has not changed. And it is surely the same within an institution. 'A state', said Burke, 'without the

[1] R. L. Orr, *The Free Church of Scotland Appeals* (1904), p. 479.

[2] *Ibid.* p. 573 (italics mine). The 'unwritten charter' corresponds to that invisible society which is the challenge to the visible.

means of some change is without the means of its conservation.' Liberty to change is necessary if we would keep alive, and there may be institutions which have denied themselves this liberty and so have become 'whited sepulchres, which indeed appear beautiful outward, but are within full of dead men's bones'.[1]

This principle which was at issue in the Scottish Churches' case applies to every group and society. In Church history it even goes back to the case of Paul of Samosata, A.D. 272. There must be within the group a self-regulating mechanism whereby the more it changes the more it remains the same. And where property is concerned it is essential that it be held on such terms as are defined by the institution itself. When Methodist union in Britain was brought about in 1932 every care was taken to safeguard these powers.

Somewhat the same kind of issue arose with regard to trade unions. The Taff Vale decision of 1901 laid down that trade unions were collectively responsible for damage done through unauthorized picketing, and so their funds were at the mercy of legal actions. This decision was reversed, after the election of 1906, by the Trade Disputes Act, but in 1908 a further issue was raised against the trade unions by the House of Lords' decision in the Osborne judgement that a trade union could not raise compulsory levies for political purposes. In 1913 a new Act represented a compromise. Members of trade unions could henceforth be exempted from political contributions if they gave due notice but otherwise the unions were free to use their funds for these purposes. The issue at the root of all these cases was whether a group of men could have freedom to act as a group responsible *as a group* for its own internal organization. Up to 1906 a trade union was looked upon simply as an association of individuals acting together for a specific purpose. It was not a community with a corporate life of its own. The Trade Disputes Act, however, was important because it gave a trade union liberty to be and to act as an organic society within the whole body politic, but it also gave liberty to individual members to follow their consciences.

[1] Matthew xxiii. 27.

Liberty and power are closely associated. Liberty means having the power to do something. It is here that crimes are done in the name of liberty, for it is power rather than liberty that is desired. As in the case of Georgi Dimitrov, it is only when power has been achieved that the nature of the claim for liberty can be assessed. This is true of groups of men as well as of individuals. A notable illustration was recently provided by the Durham County Council, which had an overwhelming Labour majority. This majority was used to try to force all employees of the Council, including doctors, to belong to an appropriate trade union or association. This is a special application of the principle known as the 'closed shop'. The move was defeated by the doctors, for although certain ranks of employment were easily replaceable if they became intransigent the doctors were not. As the Labour majority were themselves in the main trade unionists and keen protagonists of 'liberty' it would appear that in this case it was power rather than liberty that was the desired object. The argument, of course, for the closed shop in industry is that those who benefit from the struggles of other people for freedom should join the ranks of the fighters. It does not quite work out in this way, for most of the fighters are dead and the advocates of the closed shop are themselves beneficiaries from other men's labours without having had to work for their benefits. But in the case of the Durham Council the Gilbertian position was that a trade union majority of employers wished their employees to form a trade union against them! It was similar to the formation some years ago within the Co-operative movement of a trade union—the Amalgamated Union of Co-operative Employees—to safeguard the interests of those employed in the co-operative stores. In the Durham situation no allowance was made for individual liberty—the very thing that was safeguarded by the Trades Union Act of 1913 in a different situation.

These cases illustrate once more that liberty is one and indivisible. There may be sectional aims, but in so far as they are merely sectional, liberty in the full sense has not yet been achieved.

## 8 BROADCASTING

In our time the progress of science has raised certain unexpected new issues in this matter. I refer to broadcasting. The question constantly crops up how much liberty should be allowed on the air to unpopular views and minority causes. Milton was all in favour of letting truth and error grapple—'who ever knew truth to be worsted in a free and open encounter?'—but in these days truth gets very little opportunity of a free and open encounter, and even if she does, error has usually got such an advantageous start that truth can do very little against it. If liberty is an ethical quality and depends on truth there can be no greater danger to liberty than propaganda. In these matters the good man as usual is at a very material disadvantage, for his goodness is shown in forswearing the use of just those weapons which the bad man finds most effective. And this happens in small things as well as great. One wonders how far television viewers in the United States ever feel that their liberty of choice is being infringed by the blatant propaganda on behalf of advertised goods.

Public opinion in these days is very largely created by wireless, and we may ask ourselves how free discussion ought to be. We in Britain have a good reputation for fair play amongst all opinions, and political talks are given by all the political parties. When a man turns on his radio set he is just as likely to hear an attack on the Government as a talk in its favour. Similarly among the denominations. The seven major denominations[1] in this country are all given their opportunity on the air, although there may be some doubt as to the exact proportioning of time among them. But what are we to say about other groups, political and religious? The B.B.C. has been markedly nervous about allowing Unitarians on the air, as if belief in the doctrine of the Trinity had somehow been written into its charter. And smaller groups—Jehovah's Witnesses, the Catholic Apostolic Church, for instance—and even larger groups such as Christian Scientists and the

[1] Anglican, Baptist, Congregationalist, Methodist, Presbyterian, Roman Catholic, Society of Friends.

sixty-three Mormon churches in Britain never get an opportunity at all. If the fear is that they would indulge in propaganda, are not talks by Roman Catholics and any of the Protestant Churches in that way propaganda? And even if we were to give free play to every group that calls itself Christian, why should we stop at that point? Are not English Mohammedans and Buddhists and the attenders at the South Place Ethical Church worthy of some consideration?

These are difficult questions and they are often asked but rarely answered. But the same principle is involved in the case of a group larger than any of these. A very great number of people in this country bet on horses and dogs and fill in football pool coupons, and these last provide a considerable revenue for the Post Office. All these people are taxpayers and pay their licences and the B.B.C. is a national service. Now why should we not have talks on how to fill in football pool coupons? I understand it is an extremely complicated business and needs hours of thought and much experience. And as to horse racing, the novels of Nat Gould and the pages of *The Sporting Life* indicate the existence of a world of technical knowledge far beyond the ken of many a first in classics or many a chairman of a company. The ordinary sports talk on events that have happened or are happening does not go far enough. Do we not want to have some Captain Heath on the air to give us tips about future winners as well as telling us how many furlongs such and such a horse went yesterday morning? There are people who feel that the racing and betting fraternity are treated very shabbily in these matters.

What is the answer? I think it lies somewhere in the region of the idea of liberty as an ethical quality, although in saying this there is always the temptation to smugness. It is also an indication of the problems that arise in British broadcasting which do not arise in America. In America time on the air is a commodity to be sold or to be withheld from sale just as the vending company chooses. As long as it does not infringe the law or offend public morality the company is free to put on the air whatever it likes. Hence the question of differential treatment of this or that group does not arise in the form in which it arises in Britain.

The lines of broadcasting in this country were laid down by John Reith, a stern Calvinistic Scotsman. He determined that broadcasting should be an influence for good, even if to do so should require what he called 'the brute force of monopoly' without which, as he said, 'the Christian religion and the Sabbath might not have had the place and protection they had'.[1] It might not be possible to make people good by Act of Parliament but Reith really believed it could be done by wireless. He had his own ideas as to what constituted goodness and they certainly would not appeal to everybody. The principle, however, seems to have been this. First of all with regard to the denominations. It is the listening community that matters rather than the denominations and the reason for having religious broadcasts at all was not that every shade of opinion should have its chance to broadcast but rather that listeners should be edified by whatever was put on the air. On these terms the major denominations have co-operated and on the whole it has worked well. A narrowly denominational view is very rarely heard; no more often than one would hear it in the course of normal church-going. In choosing speakers and services the general acceptability to the great number of listeners is the chief consideration. It is no doubt possible that some groups would feel themselves to have not so much one contribution to make as the *only* contribution, and the period might be used for advertisement. Moreover it has been pointed out that it is of the genius of Christianity, or at any rate of Protestantism, to foster self-criticism, and criticism of the Church has been as severe from within as from without. This is a healthy attitude, and even the Roman Church by coming into the same scheme with Anglicans and Free Churchmen has for the time being at any rate laid aside its claim to infallibility. But associations which are definitely propagandist such as Jehovah's Witnesses or the Rationalist Press Association might be expected to come on the air only to further their own particular cause. There

[1] J. C. W. Reith, *Into the Wind* (1949), p. 100.

would be no body of experience and thought common to themselves and the main religious denominations which they could expound at the same level. If all this was made clear and they accepted it and the B.B.C. accepted their assurance that they would avoid propaganda, the question of inviting them to broadcast would be only a matter of fitting them in. After all, the Society of Friends is widely removed from most other forms of Christianity, but the Quakers understand these principles behind broadcasting and accept them, and no problem arises.

The question of betting news is not quite on the same level. Betting is not a sin except in so far as all attempts to get something for nothing and to make money from other people's losses are sins—but, while no one can prevent a man putting money on a horse, it is quite a different matter for a government service to help him to do so. And there is an uncomfortable feeling among most people that somehow betting is wrong even though it is not easy to say where it is wrong or why it is wrong. The fact that it so often seems to need an apology from betting people themselves by the use of an affected casualness—'just a flutter'—would seem to point in that direction. These sentiments were very much in evidence when the British Government decided to raise revenue by encouraging the purchase of Premium Bonds.

## 9 THE CHURCH AND POLITICS

In all these matters the question continually arises—what has the Church to do with politics? I have tried here and there to indicate a few principles which are Christian and which seem to me to be applicable in politics and social life. In so far as they are Christian they are necessarily part of the concern of Christian people. But here again, the distinction between the Churches as institutions and the Church as an invisible ideal comes in. The Churches as institutions represent certain taxpayers on their religious side. As taxpayers the members belong to different political parties and will no doubt vote in different ways. In the local government election in Rome in May 1956, the official organ of the Vatican, *L'Osservatore*

*Romano*, instructed the voters to vote for the Christian Democratic party, which it declared was 'the cause of God, of the Church, and of the consciences not merely of men and citizens but of believers'.[1] This from the political point of view was an interference with the voters' liberty, and it also identified religion with only one of the various political parties. Here the Church was not above the battle but actually taking sides. What then is the difference between this attitude and that of every Church in South Africa which opposes apartheid? Surely this, that the first showed concern only for the Church itself and its worldly welfare as an institution. The other represents a concern for the rights of man, quite irrespective of what might happen to the Church as an institution. If liberty is one and indivisible it clearly must apply all round—to black and white, Catholic and non-Catholic, Conservative and Labour. It must also apply to the group in the company of other groups, and to the individual in the company of other individuals within the group. The Church is continually hampered by its dual position. As an institution it is concerned about its property rights, its prestige, its power, like every other institution. Yet it has also to act in a way above the institution, as the conscience of the community, and to recognize that the institution is under judgement like every other. A significant attitude to controversial questions was shown by Archbishop William Temple in the darkest days of the economic slump of the 'thirties. Writing to *The Times* he pointed out that the greatest evil and bitterest injury of the unemployed was 'the spiritual grievance of being allowed no opportunity of contributing to the general life and welfare of the community'.[2] He incurred the wrath of Neville Chamberlain, the Chancellor of the Exchequer, for urging that the unemployed should have first claim on any surplus in the national budget, and that the restoration of 'cuts' to the unemployed should take precedence over every other form of tax remission. This, said Chamberlain, was a case of the Church 'interfering' in matters which it did not understand! However,

[1] *The Times*, 17 May 1956.

[2] F. A. Iremonger, *William Temple* (1948), p. 440.

the late Lord Keynes might be taken as an example of a man who *did* understand these things, even in Chamberlain's own interpretation of the word. And, writing to William Temple, this is what he said:

Along one line of origin at least economics, more properly called political economy, is a side of ethics.... There are practically no issues of policy as distinct from technique which do not involve ethical considerations. If this is emphasized, the right of the Church to interfere in what is essentially a branch of ethics becomes even more obvious.[1]

[1] *Ibid.* pp. 438–9.

CHAPTER IX

# THE STATE ESTABLISHMENT OF RELIGION

## 1 THE ISSUE OF ESTABLISHMENT

The question of the official recognition of religion by the State, whether in the form of an 'established' Church or by State grants, raises an acute issue in the relations of Church and State and also in the relation of denominations to one another. In England and in Scotland there are 'established' Churches, though of two different kinds. Sweden has an established Church. German churches are subsidized by the State. In the United States there is no establishment and no grants and the separation of Church and State is written into the Constitution.

## 2 THE CATHOLIC ATTITUDE[1]

'Establishment' in Catholic countries has an entirely different meaning from that in Protestant countries. The Roman Church prefers to establish itself by means of concordats, which are of the nature of treaties between two contracting parties. The effect of this is to treat the Church as a political institution.[2]

The new concordat with Spain is a good example. It is interesting that, although it was signed on 27 August 1953, it was not disclosed until *after* the military agreement with the United States on 26 September. Had it been disclosed beforehand there would undoubtedly have been strong objections to the military agreement both in the United States and in Spain itself, where the Falangists looked to the military pact to strengthen their position against the more orthodox and traditional Carlists.[3] By the con-

[1] See also appendix II, p. 183.
[2] See above, p. 10.
[3] *The Christian Century*, 26 May 1954.

cordat Franco became an ecclesiastical dignitary, 'Most Reverend' as well as 'Most Excellent'! The Vatican gave him the Order of Christ, thus following the precedent of Mussolini. The appointment of all Spanish ecclesiastic authorities from canons to the primate was placed in his hands, but priests and prelates were exempted from the ordinary legal procedures. The associations of Spanish Catholic Action were put under the immediate supervision of the hierarchy, and as these associations could now be organized for political action it meant a transfer of power if not of sovereignty from the State to the Church. The concordat affirmed that Catholicism is the only religion of the Spanish people, and even its mild statement that no one may be molested on account of his religion was denounced by the hierarchy as having no validity. Cardinal Segura y Saenz, late Archbishop of Seville, included Protestantism with atheism and Communism as 'among other grave dangers which perhaps are more to be feared because they inspire less horror'. Consequently Spanish Protestants (there are only 25,000 of them) continue to labour under grave injustices. They cannot hold any official position in the Government nor can they be officers in the army. They may not practise their faith in public. Their chapels may not advertise their existence even with a notice board nor can they be listed in the public directories. Marriage and baptism by Protestant clergy have no legal recognition. The dead cannot be interred in church cemeteries and have often to be buried in an open field. Church calendars may not be sent by post. In a village near Valladolid eighteen Protestants were put in jail for holding a secret prayer meeting and fined the equivalent of two months' pay.[1]

By the concordat the State agrees to finance everything that is needed in the formation of new dioceses, and for various other church uses. Churches, clergy residences, convents, seminaries, the buildings belonging to Catholic Action, church income and funds are all to enjoy sweeping exemption from taxation. The Church was given the right to supervise television and radio programmes. Missionary religious orders are to receive subsidies.

[1] Reported in *Time* magazine, New York, 7 March 1949.

The Government will maintain the Spanish College in Rome. Franco will contribute 8000 gold pesetas to the Holy See.

This is 'establishment' after the Roman pattern. It is not surprising that the setting-up of this theocratic State has produced widespread cynicism as well as protest. The Basques, who are earnest Catholics, have utterly rejected this 'form of Caesarism'. The situation is thus summed up by an American writer:

> The Concordat's provisions relating to the material gains of the Church set the clock back more than a century. They undid the work of the eighteenth century Charles III and Alfonso XIII's liberal minister Canalejas, who for his temerity died at the hands of an assassin. Canalejas and Charles III had both worked to lighten the burden imposed on the nation's economy by the Church's vast holdings of buildings and lands. This burden is once more saddled on the people.[1]

## 3 CHURCHES IN THE UNITED STATES AND IN SWEDEN

The separation of Church and State in the United States was first formally decreed by the Statute of Virginia in 1786. Despite the terms of the Constitution, established churches lingered on in the various States until 1833, when the establishment of the Congregational Church of Massachusetts finally came to an end. The churches in this regard are now all on a level and nowadays it would be quite impossible even in a single state for one church to be established and the others not. Perhaps the nearest approach to an established church is the position of Mormonism in Utah, but even there there can be only the feeling of establishment which comes from the fact that the greater number of inhabitants of the state are Mormons. It is not unlike the position of Roman Catholics in Spain, with the great difference that Mormons are a tolerant people and Spanish Catholics quite certainly are not. In federal affairs in America there is no one with the status of an Archbishop of Canterbury to act as religious mentor to the Government, as for instance Randall Davidson during the General Strike in 1926.[2] Congress chooses its chaplains in turn from the

[1] *Christian Century*, 26 May 1954. The article is by Lawrence Fernsworth.

[2] See above, p. 27.

chief religious communions. The point of having chaplains at all is an indication that while religion is not established it may be assumed that it is not *dis*-established. The Church receives no subsidies from the Government even for its schools (as we have in England) but Church property is exempt from taxation and this includes also private schools and colleges, most of which have a religious foundation.[1] The State recognizes the position of the conscientious objector to military service as it does in England, even though this is a tenet of none of the larger churches and must therefore be set down to the credit of this 'invisible' Church of which we have already spoken. In the absence of a royal house the symbol of American loyalty is the flag; and in the laws of seventeen states, school-children are required to salute the flag. Yet when Jehovah's Witnesses refused to conform to what they called an act of idolatry the Supreme Court, overruling not only local decisions but even its own earlier decision, declared such saluting was not legally enforceable, and the children of Jehovah's Witnesses returned to school and ignored the national symbol.

At the opposite extreme to this (apart from Roman Catholic countries) is Sweden, where Lutheranism is the established Church by a 'fundamental law' of 1809. The king and members of his councils must be members of it, and also a number of other officials including teachers. Despite laws in 1860 and 1873 which gave a measure of toleration to dissenters it was still not possible to leave the established Church unless one entered another Christian community and one which was registered. This continued until as recently as 1952, since when it has been possible to exercise free choice in these matters provided one has one's release in a document signed by the parish minister. Free Church ministers can now solemnize marriages but to do this they need the special authorization of the Government. Roman Catholics are also allowed to found monasteries but they require the Government's consent. The State controls the finances of the established

[1] The late Dr Willard L. Sperry, Dean of Divinity at Harvard, from whose excellent book *Religion in America* these facts are taken, points out (p. 61) that in Cambridge, Mass., a city whose main industry seems to be higher education, 47% of real property is exempt from tax.

Church and there is a separate Church budget. The Lutheran clergy are treated as State officials and their salaries are regulated by the Government. They are nominated by the diocesan chapter and by the appropriate State officials, who together send forward three names from which the people of the parish select one. The Church Assembly has a limited right of veto on laws which concern the Church alone, but the Government joins with it in regulating questions of liturgy.[1]

## 4 THE CHURCH OF ENGLAND

The establishment in England is more a matter of tradition than of positive law, even though it goes back to the reign of Elizabeth I, and the phrase runs, 'the Church as by law established'. Laws concerning the relations of Church and State—such as the Clarendon Code of 1660–2—have arisen out of the establishment, rather than been the basis of it. It is quite unlike the established Church of Sweden for there is no section of the budget that has to do with the Church and the Church receives no subsidies at all. The grants made to it in regard to schools are precisely on the same level as grants to schools of other denominations and to the State schools themselves. The clergy are in no sense paid servants of the State.

The marks of the establishment are many. First there is the coronation of the sovereign by the Archbishop of Canterbury. (It was interesting that at the Queen's coronation for the first time a part was taken by the head of the other established church in these islands—the Moderator of the Church of Scotland.) The Church is represented in the Upper House of Parliament by the bishops. Sentences of ecclesiastical courts are enforced by the State. The parish churches and the cathedrals are the property of the Church. Appointments to bishoprics and deaneries are made by the sovereign acting on the advice of the Prime Minister according to a peculiar form known as the *congé d'élire* whereby the chapter is allowed to elect the person whom the sovereign

[1] Article by Archbishop Brilioth of Sweden in *The Frontier*, March 1952.

has already approved, and the person elected has to take the oath of allegiance to the sovereign. Any changes in the Church's liturgy, such as were proposed in the Revised Prayer Book in 1928, have to receive the sanction of Parliament. To Parliament also the Commission on Church Finance has to present its report. The summoning of Convocation is by royal writ, and the Privy Council is in Church matters the final court of appeal.

All this looks extremely formidable, but in actual practice the Church has a very great deal of freedom. Theoretically and legally it is possible for a Baptist Prime Minister (e.g. Lloyd George) to present to the sovereign his nominations to Anglican bishoprics, but while this is a stone of stumbling and rock of offence to the Anglo-Catholic party it is noticeable that by custom the Prime Minister consults a number of representative churchmen on these matters. If unfortunate choices at times are made they might have been made equally badly by a committee of bishops. The really unedifying part of the business is that a parliament of politicians should discuss the terms in which the Church should offer its prayers to God and should have the power to reject the Church's own desires in this matter. This certainly needs revision.

There is a good deal to be said for the view that if the Church were disestablished it would be a good deal less free than it is today.[1] In theory it is very much part of the State, whereas in practice it can pretty well go its own way. As a disestablished body it would come under the laws that apply to all voluntary bodies and it would be for the courts to decide whether this or that proposal was in harmony with its trust deed. Disestablishment, which was a great Liberal and Nonconformist rallying cry fifty years ago, evokes singularly little enthusiasm today among the Free Churches who on the whole prefer things as they are. Many Anglo-Catholics, scandalized by the State connexion, would like to see the Church disestablished, but it is to be feared that if this happened it would become not one church but several. An established church ought to be, what the Church of England no doubt is, comprehensive, and any attempt to sink it to the

[1] Archbishop Cyril Garbett, *Church and State in England* (1951), p. 145.

level of a sect would be of no benefit to the country whatever. Moreover the prestige of the Church of England as an established church extends far beyond this country and far beyond its own communion. Disestablishment would be looked upon throughout the world as a national repudiation of Christianity.

There are many ways of retaining the establishment and yet allowing some self-government. The 'Life and Liberty' campaign started by William Temple in 1917 resulted in the setting-up of the Church Assembly which is a far more lively and effective as well as popular body than Convocation. It provides a more democratic instrument for discussion and proposed legislation and has succeeded to some extent in bridging the gap between the higher and the 'inferior' clergy, and between the Church and the people. The established Church of Scotland has an even greater official freedom. It is based on the Act of Union of 1929 which emphatically declares in Article 4 that the State connexion does not do away with the freedom of the Church, and Article 8 details the procedure to be adopted in changing the articles without recourse to Parliament. A great deal has been learned from the famous case of 1903–4.

These various forms of establishment show in every case a development in favour of liberalizing the institution. Ultimately this is only possible because of the theological basis that underlies it. The Roman Church could not make such adjustments without giving away its whole position.

The existence of the established Church of England brings with it some problems of relationship to other churches. Passengers on the Cunard liners will have noticed that in the prayer-book in use by the fleet the prayers of the congregation are besought for the President of the United States as well as the Queen of England. This no doubt is as it should be, although the Queen's name appears as the head of the Church of England whereas the President has no similar position in America.

On the inauguration in March 1957 of the Gold Coast as the new state of Ghana an Anglican priest, Bernard Clements, with a certain lack not only of taste but also of realism, wrote to *The*

*Times* suggesting that as the Queen was head of the state of Ghana and was also head of the established Church of England therefore the established Church of England should be also the established Church of Ghana. It was pointed out to the editor of *The Times* (who nevertheless refused to print the letter) that since the Queen was also head of the established Church of Scotland, and since there is a flourishing Scottish Presbyterian Church in Ghana, therefore the established Church of Scotland might equally well be considered as the established Church of Ghana. Although the editor ignored the Presbyterian protest, he nevertheless printed an entirely irrelevant letter from a Roman Catholic pointing out that there were far more Roman Catholics in Ghana than members of any other church (the word 'member' being, of course, undefined). The inference that was left to be drawn was that it would be grossly unfair if Anglicanism became the established religion of Ghana. If, however, numbers are to be the only test, the religion at the moment which characterizes the vast majority of the new State is animism, although it is doubtful if Dr Nkrumah and his cabinet would be impressed by this or by any other of these arguments.

The development of the State into 'Society' is paralleled in England by the way in which the Church of England is shedding some of its exclusiveness and is recognizing the place of the Free Churches in the body politic. It is this which largely accounts for the lack of enthusiasm among the Free Churches for disestablishment. At the coronation the heads of the Free Churches had their place in the procession in Westminster Abbey. The divinity degrees at Oxford and Cambridge have now long been open to Free Churchmen and most of the Divinity professorships are tenable by non-Anglicans. The term 'Nonconformist' is passing out of currency and even the term 'Dissenter', which is an offence to high-church Methodists as well as to Anglicans, is very rarely used. Yet with singular ineptitude the B.B.C. in arranging twelve broadcasts to the American churches during the war began by suggesting six Anglicans, two Romans, and four among the Free Churches and the established Church of Scotland! This showed complete ignorance of the relative strength of the different churches in America where there is no establishment at all, but it was not at all characteristic of Anglican leaders. The present Archbishop of Canterbury in a famous sermon in Cambridge in 1946 seemed to visualize bringing into the Establishment all those Free Churches that were willing to 'take episcopacy into their system', a proposal which would have delighted the heart of the great Dr Arnold of Rugby who longed for it in his day. The corollaries that follow from this new attitude will be discussed when we come to our final chapter.

The compliment is not always returned. The 'Liberation Society', whose aim is to secure the disestablishment of the Church of England, still produces propaganda for a diminishing clientele. And still more remarkably a recent book by J. S. Whale on the Protestant Tradition ignores completely and apparently of set purpose the part played by Anglicanism in the formation of that tradition—if indeed tradition is the right word.[1]

[1] See above, p. 25.

# CHAPTER X

# EQUALITY

## I THE MIRAGE OF EQUALITY

As a prelude to a consideration of equality let us hear the preamble to the American Declaration of Independence.

When in the course of human events it becomes necessary for one people to dissolve the political bands which have connected them with another, and to assume among the powers of the earth the separate and equal station to which the Laws of Nature and of Nature's God entitle them, a decent respect to the opinions of mankind requires that they should declare the causes which impel them to the separation.

We hold these truths to be self-evident, that all men are created equal, that they are endowed by their Creator with certain inalienable rights, that among these are life, liberty and the pursuit of happiness.

These two paragraphs illustrate the fascination that the idea of equality has always had for mankind. It will be noted that the colonists declare that they are not only separate from all other communities but they are also equal to them and the one is as important as the other. Yet it is a strange claim to make, for equality is one of those attributes which are entirely in the gift of other people. It is not the claim that constitutes equality, but the granting of it. To ask for it is a confession of one's own inequality, for why should a man claim equality from someone else who is inferior or already equal to him? It can be claimed only from someone recognized rightfully or wrongfully to be superior. Moreover in this context it will be noted that equality is claimed only for a particular group against other groups. It is not concerned about the individuals within the group. In this matter the founding fathers might have been embarrassed. Slaves lived in the cellars of the country houses of many of them, for it was clear that while God may have created all men equal some of them, as the saying is, were more equal than others. The Stoic rationalism of the Declaration did not necessarily apply underground.

And then again, is it true that men were created equal? In what ways are they equal? They are certainly not equal in physical strength, in appearance, in temperament, in ability, in aptitudes, in wisdom, in spiritual sensitiveness and in a score of other ways. Nor are they equal in colour or race. And history shows two ways of dealing with these inequalities. One is to stereotype them by associating with them yet further inequalities, as for instance in the case of women whose progress towards emancipation has been loaded with inequalities of every kind, in law, in property rights, in the franchise, in wages and in many other ways. The other movement has been by seeking to remove these inequalities and to enable men to be equal.

From the days of John Ball and the rising of the Kentishmen those who have insisted on the equality of men in their creation have sought support in the Bible.

When Adam delved and Eve span
Who was *then* the gentleman?

But these simple souls might have found more suitable texts in the New Testament, where it is emphasized that in Christ there is neither Jew nor Greek, male nor female, bond nor free, but all are one in Him. At the same time it is in the Epistles that we discover that even in Christ people are as unequal in function from one another as the hand and the foot, the ear and the eye, and as unequal in gifts as apostles, prophets, pastors, healers, interpreters and teachers. It is clear therefore that what the Bible is here talking about is not inequality at all but difference. And these differences persist, whatever we may do about it. They can be made the basis of equality or of inequality whichever we choose. To make them a basis of inequality is easy, for the lines are already laid down. But to make them the basis of equality requires a creative act and that act cannot take place except within a community committed to the mutual appreciation of differences. In other words the pattern of equality in human relations is not that of a lot of eggs in a basket, all exactly alike, but of a family bound together by love and respect. It is within a family that differences and equality most naturally co-exist. God creates men different and at the same time of equal value in his sight and the Church is meant to follow that pattern. Equality is not a claim to be made, it is a fact to be demonstrated.

## 2 PRIVATE PROPERTY

It is in economic matters that the question of equality becomes most controversial and for many people the equality of property and income is the only kind of equality in which they are interested. The difference between the 'haves' and the 'have nots' is the most obvious difference of all. Before discussing equality and inequality, therefore, we must first look at the case for private property.

In spite of the increasing regard for persons by the most progressive communities it is nevertheless true that penalties imposed by the law-courts for offences against persons are often far lighter than for offences against property. The right emphasis, however, is quite clear when we look at the New Testament. Riches are a snare. Only with immense difficulty can a rich man enter the kingdom of heaven—a remark of Jesus which caused the disciples to exclaim 'Who then can be saved?' The Temple buildings which earned the rapturous admiration of the disciples counted as nothing to Jesus in comparison with human issues. Persons are clearly of more account than property.

Is the principle, however, as clear from the point of view of the ideal society?

In the case of the individual the justification for private property is that it is an extension of personality. To have no private property at all is to sink in the scale of humanity. In the Middle Ages, and perhaps also since then, the voluntary poverty of the individual monk was often compensated by the wealth of the monastery as a corporate body. When the Abbot of Cluny, who was vowed to poverty, went on progress around his dependent houses he took with him a retinue of nine hundred people. Where property is held by a corporation like this it is really held in trust, and it is argued that, while an individual requires no more property than will enable him to do his work properly and contribute his best to the life of the community, the same principle does not hold good of trustees for property that is not their individual possession. Again, what would have been the heritage for future generations had the builders of the medieval cathedrals and colleges considered that persons were of more account than property? There are obviously many sides to this question, but if we remember that society means past and future as well as present, and if we remember too that concern for persons includes concern for their spiritual and intellectual well-being, we shall find that the principle still holds good.

We have to draw a distinction between that measure of private property which is required by a man to enable him to give his best to the community and that measure which is over and above this, especially if it gives him power over the lives of other men. There is a distinction between property for use and property for power.

The distinction, however, is not easy to draw when we consider private property the use of which has been postponed or forgone. This of course is what we mean in the simplest sense by 'capital'. Capital is a necessary factor in the development of industry and the fact that in the past it has been so closely associated with exploitation does not mean that exploitation is an inevitable accompaniment. A good deal—indeed everything—depends on who holds the capital, who is going to benefit from it, and what is the extent of the payment to be made for its use.

A certain well-known religious newspaper is owned by shareholders, to each of whom is allotted no more than one £100 share. For this he receives interest at the rate of 10% free of tax. He may not, however, sell his share, give it away or bequeath it. If he has no further use for it it returns to the company to be re-allotted by them to someone else. Apart from the handsome—too handsome—dividend this would seem to be a way of so controlling capital as to avoid the odium of giving it power over the lives of men.

The general question of interest is a serious one. In the production of commodities a large dividend can be paid only by keeping the price far beyond the cost of production or by paying the workers far below their value to the company or by an inadequate insurance against risk or by a combination of all three. Profit-sharing, however, is no solution, for it keeps the accruing benefits within the ring of the concern itself. The man left out is the most important man of all, the consumer.

The present levelling of incomes, the guaranteeing of pension, health and unemployment benefits, and the emphasis on property for use have had a serious effect on incentive. Unless a man can have some guarantee that he will be able to enjoy the fruits of his labour in a way which he himself approves he will be disinclined to do more than is absolutely necessary. On the other hand if after all these and other benefits have been paid for out of income tax and other taxes the entire surplus is at a person's own discretion to use as he likes we have once more the principle that a man may do what he likes with his own, regardless of social consequences. This is the capitalist system upside down. Whereas, therefore, a generation or so ago the Church came to be greatly exercised about profits, ought it not now to be greatly concerned about earnings? Whereas once the Christian principle that was held to be relevant within the capitalist system was 'the stewardship of wealth', ought there not now to be a 'stewardship of wages'? And as the well-to-do believers in the stewardship of wealth were concerned with how it was spent rather than how it was earned, ought there not in these days of the decline of the capitalist system to be equal inquiry into how wages are both earned and spent?

One further problem arises in this context. Let us take as an illustration the great John Rylands Library in Manchester or the Huntington Library in California, two of the most notable benefactions that have ever been made to learning. They both arose out of private property; the owners preferred to spend their money in this way to the benefit of scholars everywhere rather than to spend it on themselves. If private property should be limited to what is of immediate use, benefactions such as these will henceforth cease and the money will have to be found either by governments or by a vast number of small donors who may well have to be educated up to it. What guarantee is there that a government would do such a thing? But even if it were willing to do so, on what grounds is it thought that a committee would be a better judge of what is needful in these matters than an enlightened private donor? And to mulct the possible donor by heavy taxation may not only prevent him playing the part of patron but may mean that his money is diverted to totally other purposes. Clearly there are some things better done by the community at large and others by individual effort and others by combining the two. An interesting example of co-operation in these matters was the arrangement by which the *Codex Sinaiticus* came to the British Museum. The Bolsheviks offered it for £100,000. Towards this the British Government gave half and the other half was raised by an incredible number of small donations from school-children, churches and private persons. A unique object like this obviously ought not to be in private hands, but the way of acquiring it was an excellent justification both of the use of public money and of the importance of private property. Since in our time the springs of charity on the large scale are apt to dry up because of the incidence of taxation the benefits of this kind of private property need to be conserved by some such method as this.

To Karl Marx value is created by labour and therefore the profits of labour should all go to the labourer. This is a naïve simplification of the situation not dissimilar from that which one may find in Aquinas and elsewhere, and Marx indeed has been described as 'the last of the Schoolmen'.[1] If, however, we are to have a sound theory and equally sound practice in regard to private property we must consider not only producers but still more consumers. The price of labour, the price of materials and the price of the article to the consumer are all involved, and it is possible that no one of these factors really corresponds to value. It is the difference between value for use and price for exchange that so often makes the holding of private property unjust.

[1] R. H. Tawney, *Religion and the Rise of Capitalism* (Penguin), p. 49.

What then is the conclusion of the whole matter? It is often said that there is no inherent right in private property, but surely if our principle is that persons take precedence over property we have to reckon with that innate and proper urge within all persons which is, so to speak, to externalize our personality in things whose possession does not deny to other men or groups of men something which is rightly theirs.

On the other hand ownership is not everything. The Romans made a useful distinction between two forms of ownership. *Dominium* was possession in the sense of absolute ownership—the millionaire's possession, for instance, of a picture. *Possessio* was ownership of a different kind—that of the art student who can go to the National Gallery as often as he likes and gaze upon his beloved Rembrandt. There are many things in the world which admit of public 'dominium' together with private 'possessio', and perhaps the more of them there are the better.

The only absolute owner is God. Whatever 'surplus value' there may be in labour it is his also, for he is the creator of all values. This reference continually had in remembrance will clear our minds of cant either about the so-called 'sacred rights of property' or about the supposed greater benefits of public ownership. Μηδὲν ἄγαν. It is excess that ruins everything and the only way to be sure of what is legitimate and what is excess is by this reference and a due consideration of all that follows from it. This is a proper function of the Church in politics. It will, however, be as much an acid test for the individual denominations as for the State. The large churches represent a vast amount of money and property, and their guardians have often taken the line of Archdeacon Grantly in Trollope's book that an attack on church revenue is an attack upon religion itself. But if the Church is to put persons before property it must be emphasized that this includes church property. The difficulty here of course is that all this is trustee ownership and not private property at all, and reform has often been withstood on the ground that while a man may be willing to give away property which is his own he cannot give away that which he holds in trust for someone else. There is truth in this, but the Church holds what it holds in trust for the spiritual and material needs of the people for whom Christ gave away everything. In this way the Church acts for the glory of God. To use the phrase 'for the glory of God' to justify action or lack of action that benefits the shepherds and is detrimental to the flock comes perilously near the Jewish habit of 'Corban' and merits the same condemnation.[1]

## 3 ECONOMIC EQUALITY

That some people have more income than they actually need while other people have less than they need is obvious. It would seem therefore that on grounds of justice some equalizing of incomes should be necessary. The revolutionary way is to take by force from the 'haves' and share it out with the 'have nots'. In Britain this act of spoliation is performed without fuss or violence by the Chancellor of the Exchequer. The following table will give some indication of the results.

CLASSIFICATION OF NET PERSONAL INCOMES
(after payment of income tax and surtax)

| Range of income (£) | Numbers of incomes in each range 1938–9 | 1945–6 | 1947–8 | 1954–5 | 1955–6 |
|---|---|---|---|---|---|
| 155–249 | 4,500,000 | 7,950,000 | 8,470,000 | 3,320,000 | 2,210,000 |
| 250–499 | 1,820,000 | 5,225,000 | 8,740,000 | 8,730,000 | 8,240,000 |
| 500–999 | 450,000 | 652,000 | 1,378,000 | 7,380,000 | 8,650,000 |
| 1000–1999 | 155,000 | 137,500 | 320,000 | 731,000 | 936,000 |
| 2000–3999 | 56,000 | 34,615 | 58,500 | 131,000 | 149,600 |
| 4000–5999 | 12,000 | 840 | 3,430 | 7,100 | 12,000 |
| 6000 | 7,000 | 45 | 70 | 200 | 600 |

This table is compiled from the figures quoted by R. H. Tawney, *Equality*, 4th ed. (1952), p. 242, together with those given in the Inland Revenue Reports for the years ended 31 March 1956 and 31 March 1957.

It will be noticed that there has been a steady move upward from the lowest-paid classes that are taxable (incomes below £155 are omitted) and a steady move downward from the highest-paid classes. At the same time, from 1947, there has been a *general* rise of income for *all* classes.

To get the *exact* position of the different classes the income figures would have to be compared with the cost of living index and the corresponding fall in the purchasing power of the £.

[1] Mark vii. 11.

It would appear highly satisfactory that the extremes of riches and poverty should be done away with, and no one in these days would defend either. And yet we can see that to take from a man receiving, say, £100,000 a year as much as nineteen-twentieths, leaving him with only £5000, might in some cases work out to the disadvantage of society. The John Rylands Library in Manchester has already been mentioned. It was opened in 1899 at a time when income tax was ninepence in the pound. In these days of heavy taxation any such gift would scarcely be possible. It might, of course, be contended that such provision for learning should be made by the State, and that while John Rylands's money was certainly put to good use it is possible—so it has been alleged—that the money ought to have gone instead into the pockets of underpaid Manchester workpeople. Yet when one sees the alcoves of that great building filled with students who are the descendants of those same workpeople making free use of the wonderful facilities provided, it is impossible not to feel that the sufferings of a previous generation have worked out for good to those who come after. This is not in the least to justify low wages, but rather a recognition of the way in which the principle of vicariousness sometimes works. The point at issue, however, is not whether the money would have been better used in the hands of the workpeople than in Rylands's hands, but whether it was better used by Rylands than it would have been by a Government department. No doubt the Cadburys, the Carnegies, the Huntingtons, the Rylands and the Andrew Mellons got considerable personal enjoyment out of this kind of power used beneficently. But this ought not to take away from the fact that their benefactions have been for the good of the community. Granted that wealth is a trust, who are to be the trustees? The equalizing of incomes by taxation may deprive of power the very people who could be guaranteed to use it wisely.

In these days, somewhat the same purpose is being served by the creation of trusts whose purpose is to do for our time what the private benefactor was able to do in the past. Most of these philanthropic trusts and foundations are American. Their advantage is that it can always be ensured that the trust will be carried on in the next generation in the same spirit as that of the founders. Private benefactors could not always ensure that their heirs and assigns would be of the same mind as themselves.

The method of Robin Hood of taking from the rich to benefit the poor needs careful watching to see that the beneficiaries are or can be really benefited. Joe Varwell, the socialist in Eden Philpotts' play *Yellow Sands*, is left £4000 and wants to give it all to the unemployed. He is horrified to find that all it would do for a million unemployed would be to give most of them a box of matches each and it would still leave 40,000 unprovided for! So with the money he builds a shelter upon the foreshore for the fishermen. Was the money therefore better used for that purpose than if it had gone in relief of the national debt?

The position at the extremes, however, is not the most difficult question. The levelling of incomes produces a completely false idea of equality. It has regard to the cash amounts received but ignores both the source of the income and the way in which it is spent. For example, a working man saves his money and invests it in a house the rent from which is to help to keep him in his old age. The rent is controlled, meaning that it is stabilized at a certain figure, no matter how the cost of living varies. In due course the amount received does not equal the cost of keeping it in repair. He cannot get more money from the tenant, he cannot sell it, he cannot give it away. And yet any attempt to interfere with that rent is looked upon by some people as a concession to those mysterious creatures called the 'capitalists'—of whom our thrifty working man is one.

But it is the way in which income is spent that creates an even more difficult problem. After the necessities of life are procured, and taxes are paid, and in days when health, unemployment and pensions are taken care of by the State, the method of spending the remainder marks the differences between mankind better than any other external sign. Some men will, and do, spend the lot. Here is the opportunity for what Veblen called 'conspicuous waste' and it is noticeable in all classes of society. The wife of a wealthy British industrialist spends money on a heavily ornate motor-car, perhaps the most expensive that has ever been made. At the other extreme many houses in poor working-class districts have their roofs festooned with television aerials. There is no incentive to save, and yet so often the money goes in attempts to get more money either to spend at once or to ensure that the owner need never work again. The attraction of a £75,000 prize from the football pools means far more to certain people than even a high salary earned by their own labour. The implication in *Genesis* that work is a curse is often the only part of the teaching of Holy Writ with which many people are familiar. A pitman in Newcastle upon Tyne was once asked what he would do if he were the Duke of Northumberland. 'I'd lie in bed all day with my top hat on', he said. Quite often when people think of equality of incomes it means an equality at that alleged level. Many people in the industrial areas do not require the State to stabilize their incomes at a certain figure, they do it for themselves. Absenteeism is directly due to the fact that many men would rather have less work than more money. This balance of work and income is upset when the cost of living rises and it is in order to restore the balance rather than merely to get more money that a rise in wages or salaries is made the object of a claim or a strike. It is interesting also to notice in many an industrial district another indication that money is not always the most desirable object. Where white-collar jobs are more esteemed than manual labour, the increase of wages for the manual job by no means guarantees that it will be preferred.

This, however, is again an extreme, for an undue love of idleness is a pathological condition. But when we take the great mass of wage and salary earners and imagine them all having equal incomes, the inequality of the total situation becomes apparent. It may and does penalize some people to the extent that they cannot afford the books or tools necessary for their job, they cannot indulge in their favourite hobbies or they cannot send their children to the schools of their choice. How are we to equate the necessary personal expenditure of a scientific worker, a clergyman, a trade union official, a journalist and a shop assistant? Each clearly needs a certain expenditure on 'tools for the job' which would not be needed by an unskilled factory worker. Yet the definition of 'tools for the job' is not always wisely left to the person concerned. Some people might think that a gold-plated high-powered car was an absolute necessity to enable them to do their work properly, and no doubt other people have had equally strange ideas of what was necessary in their case. But the differences are nevertheless present. At the present price of books it is not unusual for a scholar to spend £100 a year on books alone. A good craftsman will want better and more expensive tools than are necessary for a purely routine job. It is interesting that facts such as these are now recognized by the income-tax authorities and a rebate is possible on books and other necessary materials for a man's work. Net incomes, therefore, in relation to the differences of occupation, have a tendency towards equality, but this is not the same thing as saying that incomes are equal. To say that they might be more nearly equalized if more use were made of public libraries and technical schools and that there is thus no need for a person to own books himself is to ignore the very real importance that a man's own tools have for a man. Cricketers have their own bats and carpenters their own favourite plane, and these are just illustrations of the need every man has for possessions that are his own and chosen by himself.

Even this, however, is not the last word. A man has to live his life as a person and not just as a bricklayer or a lawyer or a bank clerk. And as a person, what is the necessary expenditure to enable him to give his best contribution to society? He may be keen on mountain climbing or bird watching or classical concerts or gardening or angling or vicarious sport, and all of these involve some expense. For such things as these no allowance can be made by the State and, while taxation may tend to keep net incomes level, expenditure on these pursuits is a necessary way of expressing individuality and difference. It is at this point that liberty and equality in economic matters cut across one another. Clearly equality which can take no account of such differences will bear more heavily on some than on others, in one case limiting their freedom and in another enhancing it.

The factor of incentive occurs again in the vexed question of differentials in industry. In order to persuade men to take on more responsible jobs, wages have to be made unequal. Make all wages alike and there will be no incentive to men to work harder, to equip themselves better, to branch out in new directions or to accept responsibility. Money being the commonest standard of value, extra money must be attached to certain types of work in order to have them taken up. Yet it does not always work in that way. Some men value the opportunity for doing craft work more than a managerial post with higher pay. Some teachers would prefer to continue as assistants rather than to get more money as a head. And in the upper reaches of the professions it often works in the opposite direction. Lawyers do not mind cutting their income to a third by exchanging the bar for the bench. Clearly no amount of juggling with money can ever really be relied upon to produce that equality which men seem to think they desire. The more we go into the question the clearer it is that once again the pattern of the family is the only really workable pattern for a free society.

The desire for equality of incomes is very largely based on the idea of labour as a commodity. The habit of absenteeism assumes that a man has this commodity to sell or to withhold from sale just as he chooses. It is one of the disheartening paradoxes of the present time that just when labour is becoming more conscious of itself as an essential partner in the community which is the State, the old habit of thinking only of rights and claims should still persist. There can never be a free society built on claims.

In a certain village in Scotland there lived at the beginning of this century a dominie of the old school and his wife. They had four sons. One became a famous missionary in Africa, one went to London, became a famous surgeon and was granted a knighthood, the third became the head of a large business and the fourth stayed at home as a jobbing gardener. At New Year time the sons always tried to get home to the village, and whenever they managed it a strange transformation took place. The eminent surgeon regained at once his old reputation for being the neatest hand in the village at mending bicycles. The business-man would sit by the hour getting sage advice from the gardener. They every one of them thought that the missionary was doing the most important job of the lot, while the missionary, who afterwards became Moderator of the Kirk, thought there was no one so accomplished in theology as his old father.

There you have difference with equality in the only kind of community in which it is possible, that of the family. It is consonant with the genius of Christianity that this should be the pattern intended by God for all human life.

## 4 POLITICAL EQUALITY

When we turn to political equality the same complication arises. If we hold to the principle of 'one man, one vote' and that 'all should count for one and none for more than one', are we thereby asserting that all men are equally capable of exercising the franchise? Before these slogans were translated into policy it was held that the political system should be weighted on the side of those who had 'a stake in the country'. They were a bulwark against any major alteration in things as they were, and whether they were Whigs or Tories they belonged to the same class of society.

Now, as we have already seen,[1] the idea of 'a stake in the country' is excellent so long as it is properly interpreted. Every citizen has a stake of some sort in the country, although it may not be property; and the greater his sense of responsibility the more he will eschew violence. But if this is to be the general principle of society, each person must recognize and appreciate the stake that other people have in the country. Each man's life and standard of living are rightly precious to him, and to assume that quantity of possessions is the only thing that matters is to take up an extraordinarily mechanical attitude to human relationships.

[1] Above, p. 79.

The principle, however, of 'one man, one vote' creates a serious problem. While counting heads is undoubtedly a better way of carrying on society than breaking them, are we sure that counting them is the best of all? How, for instance, are we going to equate the importance to the country of a Teddy boy who makes a nuisance of himself in the streets and that of a skilled surgeon or an engineer or a school-teacher? It is not the people in themselves we are comparing, for we do not have the means to do that, but their value as voters. If a majority composed of Teddy boys held the franchise, political power would be put into the hands of those least fitted to use it, and governments might be put in or turned out for no real reason at all. While votes may be all equal, what the votes represent may be widely different. And in this regard a mechanical equality may mean a serious threat to liberty.

Various devices have been used to safeguard the security of the State against irresponsible voters. One is plural voting. This again was based on property and not therefore easy to defend. There was more to be said for the university vote, had it been exercised on other than party lines: so many of the members chosen might equally well have represented any ordinary constituency. A person such as Miss Eleanor Rathbone was the ideal university member and was genuinely independent of merely party interests. Yet if one particular group are to have their voting power weighted in this way, why not other groups as well?

The device favoured in Russia and elsewhere is to distribute voting power, not according to territorial divisions, but according to occupations. The members represent interests rather than areas. This is partly true of the British House of Lords. The Lords include representatives of the law, the Church, politics, science, medicine, literature, administration, business and other interests in the country. This to many people's way of thinking is its final justification and it is a useful device to have one house elected on a territorial basis and the other on a quite different principle.

Unfortunately there are two main objections in practice. The first is the hereditary principle. It may be useful to have an eminent scientist in the Lords to represent the interests of science. But there is no guarantee that his eldest son will do the same, any more than that the present Duke of Wellington is the man to be commander-in-chief of the British Army. Secondly, the great majority of the House of Lords does not represent any interests except land-owning, big business and purely political concerns, and these peers owe their seats solely to the hereditary principle. Thus the House of Lords tends to become simply another House of Commons, an assembly of politicians, but having no constituency to which they are periodically responsible.

The hereditary principle, moreover, has the same influence as the right of bequest. Nothing maintains inequality so much as uncontrolled right of bequest. It enables selected members of the next generation to start where their predecessors left off, not because of any superior ability or deeper sense of responsibility but by the accident of being beneficiaries under a will. It is not surprising therefore that the move to level out incomes by taxation has been accompanied by limitations if not on the right of bequest at any rate on its results. Sometimes such limitations have been almost punitive and unjust, as when by the accident of an heir's death soon after his entry on his estate two lots of death duties are payable within the matter of a year or two. The incidence of death duties and other such taxes has brought with it a very material alteration in the holding of property. Large mansions are more and more passing into the hands of corporate, often statutory, bodies which alone are able to maintain them, and the 'stately homes of England' have their peace disturbed by the shouting of school-children or the scratching of the pens of civil servants.

Some limitations are also made in the operation of the hereditary principle even in the case of the House of Lords. Judges become life peers, and of course the bishops do not hold their seats by hereditary right. An extension of this practice, whereby the House of Lords is separated from the peerage, might keep all the advantages of the present system with none of its drawbacks.

Proportional representation has been advocated as a means of securing a more genuine representation of the country in Parliament. It has the advantage of an appearance of justice on mathematical lines, but very serious difficulties arise in practice. It stabilizes the situation at a given time on the assumption that all Conservatives vote Conservative all the time and all Labour vote Labour all the time, and the same with Liberals. Moreover, it does not overcome the difficulty about the Teddy boys, for it assumes again that all voting is by conviction and attachment to a party. It has been commonly said at all elections from 1945 onwards that the great majority of English voters are Liberal at heart although under our present system the results of the polls do not show it. But the aim of an election is to put in power a government that can run the country. There is, of course, no absolute guarantee of this even under the present system but it is more likely to happen than under a system which is assumed to register merely political loyalties. There is no situation more unsatisfactory than to have a government in office but not really in power, holding on precariously by continual compromise with this or that group of dissidents. The kaleidoscopic changes of government in France are not an inspiring example. Although at any given time or at any given election the results in Britain may show great discrepancies between the feelings of the country and the strength of the government elected, nevertheless over a period of years the net result is more representative and certainly more effective than if all elections were held on mathematical lines.

It is clear that no administrative device can really create political equality. Indeed many devices result not in equality but in irresponsibility. The claim for liberty is often a disguised claim for power. The same is on occasion true of the claim for equality.

## 5 EQUALITY AND LIBERTY. DE TOCQUEVILLE

Before we leave the question of political equality it will be well to consider its relations to political liberty.

It has often been held that liberty and equality are antagonistic ideas. If there is equality, i.e. of status, of income, of political and property rights, it is clear that some people are being cramped of the opportunity to give their best to society and others are given more opportunity than their abilities can compass, and so liberty is impossible. On the other hand, if there is liberty there must be liberty to be different, and therefore equality is impossible. Clearly there is some confusion in all this, and it arises from isolating the individual from the setting in which he finds himself and even isolating certain aspects of the individual's life from others. It cannot be too often emphasized that the study of human nature is an *ecological* study—that is, it is concerned with men in relation to their environment. This includes a great variety of relationships, of mind and body, thought and emotion, motive and action, and the relationship of a man to his family, his occupation, his local group, and the physical and spiritual conditions of his life. To take an arbitrary selection from these in order to bring about equality with another man is bound to result in an infringement of liberty.

The classic treatment of the relationship of liberty and equality is to be found in de Tocqueville's *Democracy in America*, one of the most remarkable books ever written.[1] It was published in 1835. He was only thirty at the time and he had paid one visit to America. Yet it is full of political wisdom and much of it is strikingly relevant to our present time since Russia moved into the orbit of the world's affairs and since we became accustomed to the omnicompetent State.

His thesis is that liberty must come before equality, and if we define liberty as the appreciation of differences and the opportunity to give one's best service to the community we shall see the wisdom of his position. He lived at a time of revolution in Europe, while in America it was a period of violent party conflicts. The conservatism of New England, the planter aristocracy of the South, the pioneer community of the West, and the new democracy growing up on the Atlantic seaboard were all struggling for power, and the election of Andrew Jackson in 1828 put into the presidential chair the most autocratic president

[1] Henry Reeves's translation (1835–40) is reprinted in the World's Classics series (Oxford) with a preface by H. S. Commager.

the United States has ever known. Every type of political opinion was at its most combative stage and young de Tocqueville had just the right type of mind to sort them all out and to present the American scene in a reasoned plan. He naturally had in mind the various revolutions through which France had passed since 1789 and was able to compare his own country with the situation in America. He saw that different countries worked out their political and social institutions in their own way. America was a laboratory of democracy and no one knew what the final result would be. Liberty and equality were both at work and the country was so vast that the antagonism between the two could not be noticed by the people most concerned. De Tocqueville, however, saw it clearly enough:

Among men who have lived free long before they became equal the habits of mind that arise from free institutions neutralize to some extent the effects of the principle of equality. And although the central authority may increase its power among such people the individuals will never entirely forfeit their independence. But when equality of conditions grows up among a people which has never known, or has long ceased to know, what freedom is (and such is the case upon the Continent of Europe) the old forms of national life become irresistibly attracted to the new ways and ideas and are blended with them. Consequently all powers seem spontaneously to rush to the centre and there they accumulate with startling rapidity. The State instantly attains the utmost limits of its strength, while individuals allow themselves to sink as suddenly to the lowest level of weakness.

He proposes, with a slight touch of cynicism, the way in which this result can be brought about: 'The foremost or, indeed, the sole condition which is required in order to succeed in centralizing the supreme power in a democratic community, is to love equality, or to get men to believe you love it.' We have seen all this happen in Communist countries, where regard for the working classes is a smoke-screen behind which a cynical minority who control the instruments of coercion seek only to maintain themselves in power. With such situations in mind we can appreciate two other remarks of de Tocqueville: 'For the principle of equality begets two tendencies: the one leads men straight to independence, and may suddenly drive them into anarchy; the other conducts them by a longer, more secret, but more certain road, to servitude.' And again, with certain reservations, and speaking of the community at large:

> Above this race of men stands an immense and tutelary power, which takes upon itself alone to secure their gratifications, and to watch over their fate. That power is absolute, minute, regular, provident, and mild. It would be like the authority of a parent, if, like that authority, its object was to prepare men for manhood; but it seeks, on the contrary, to keep them in perpetual childhood: it is well content that the people should rejoice, provided they think of nothing but rejoicing. For their happiness such a government willingly labours, but it chooses to be the sole agent and the only arbiter of that happiness.

Events in Europe since the last war provide a sufficient comment.

## 6 EQUALITY IN EDUCATION

My last illustration of the workings of the principle of equality is education. Education is an influence which can be made to work in two quite contrary directions. Dealing, as it is bound to do, with the differences among men, it can build on those differences either a system of equality or a system of inequality. Education even brings to light differences that were never before suspected. This happens no matter what the ultimate aim of education may be, for the new material of education blends with the minds of men and produces a different result in every case, since the minds of no two men are exactly alike. Nevertheless equality in education has for long been an aim of social reformers. It is sometimes called 'equality of opportunity', which is an excellent principle at the beginning of the process as long as it is not expected to produce equality at the other end. For 'equality of opportunity' has about it an almost grudging spirit of competition and it is genuinely believed that this is the road to a classless society and to an equality even more desirable than equality of income. It goes with other slogans of a similar nature—such as 'there's plenty of room at the top' and 'get on or get out'.

It carries us back to the days of Samuel Smiles, although Smiles did not ask help from anybody. He believed in self-help and in people creating their own opportunities. It is just possible that the welfare state, having attempted to give an equal education to all, has now discovered that no system on earth can create ability if it is not there, and that equality of opportunity has clogged the wheels of higher education with numbers of people who have not the ability to profit by it.

The real whipping boy in the English system of education is the public school.[1] It is, with some truth, considered to be the chief cause of inequality among the classes of the English people. Here we have in England a national system of education provided for all children aged from five to fifteen and beyond it to eighteen, and right alongside this system is another, paid for by private persons and by endowments, which trains a select class (a selection based not on ability but on money and position). The two systems work on lines which never meet until the products come together as masters and men in business or as fellow students in the universities. How galling this must be—and is—to planners and egalitarians and communists and many more who would, if they could, enjoy such a system for themselves! This is the line of argument and it is associated with jests about the old school tie and the number of Old Etonians in the Cabinet. Sometimes, by an understandable paradox, it is old public school men themselves who are the chief critics of the public schools.

I wonder, however, whether this is not representative of a state of things that is passing away. The golden age of the English public schools was when Thring was at Uppingham and Arnold's methods had become orthodox. The classic statement about the social function of the English public schools will be found in volume I of the Report of the Clarendon Commission in 1864. This is the relevant paragraph:

> It is not easy to estimate the degree in which the English people are indebted to these schools for the qualities on which they pique themselves most—for their capacity to govern others and control them-

[1] See above p. 92, note.

selves, their aptitude for combining freedom with order, their public spirit, their vigour and manliness of character, their strong but not slavish respect for public opinion, their love of healthy sport and exercise.... They have had perhaps the largest share in moulding the character of an English gentleman (p. 56).

After reading this all we can say, with Gilbert and Sullivan, is

Bow, bow, ye lower middle classes,
Bow, bow, ye tradesmen, bow ye masses!

In days when education is a civil right and is recognized as such by the United Nations' Declaration of Human Rights, it would seem that these distinctions should be done away by bringing the public schools into the national system and making them available to children of merit from whatever class they come. This is alleged to be the happy situation in America where schools like Groton and Hotchkiss count for much less in American life than do the English schools of similar type in the life of England.

This of course is the argument from equality, and it is based on the plain fact that the attractiveness of the public school for many people is not in the least due to an assessment of its educational excellence but because it gives a social *cachet* not obtainable even at a much-better-equipped Council (or, as it is called nowadays in England, County) school. We have already noted the administrative characteristics of the English public school. It is a peculiarly English product, credited by some to Dr Arnold of Rugby, by others to the system which as a boy he found at Winchester, and by others to Thring of Uppingham. What is called a 'public' school in America is a school that is really owned by the public and which therefore corresponds to our Council or County schools. The English Council school (like the American public school) has no fees, while the people who send their sons and daughters to public schools have to pay fees themselves and also are taxed for the upkeep of the Council schools. This is sometimes looked upon as a grievance and people used to grumble at having to educate what they called 'other people's children'; but it is a situation voluntarily accepted and maintained by those who feel it worth while in order that their family can keep up a desired position in society. As long therefore as people are willing to pay the price there seems no reason why they should not go on doing so. Indeed to prevent them from doing so would be to come down on the side of equality against liberty.

It is noticeable, however, that the public schools have set the pace for the Council schools, partly from a slavish copying of the externals of the system—houses, prefects, blazers, caps and mottoes—but partly also because, when the purely snobbish considerations are left out of account, the public school exhibits certain sound educational principles and methods. The levelling down of the public schools might easily eliminate much more than snobbery: it might have an adverse effect on education as a whole. All education costs money and it is not always easy to get a local authority to spend money on what might be called the imponderables in education, while it is easier to spend money on buildings and equipment. The imponderables in this case arise from the easy relations of senior boys and masters and this is largely made possible by the intimacy of small classes. We find a development in two directions. The County grammar schools aim more and more at a large sixth form and small classes, and thus move towards the public school, while the public schools are developing along more democratic lines by giving scholarships for boys from the Council schools. This last device to counteract the evils of the class system and to make for a greater equality does not always work. It has already been pointed out that all human relationships have in them an ecological element, that is to say a mutual connexion with their environment. To uproot a boy from his environment and place him in a different type of society may create a dissociation which is positively harmful. Every individual is the centre of a complex of associations and to treat him simply as an isolated individual is to ignore the pull of circumstances. Equality in one direction may lead to a greater inequality in another. Accordingly the desired results are much more likely to be attained by reproducing in the Council schools the curricula, the type of discipline and the organization of the timetable of the public schools, not all of them boarding schools, than by experimenting with a few individuals. And indeed this is happening. The classical tradition is moving into the County schools and the science tradition is finding a place in the public schools. A few years ago a municipal boys' grammar school in a Lancashire cotton town well known to the writer was discovered to have 400 pupils, of whom ninety were in the sixth form and fifty of whom were learning Greek. Yet this had not been to the disadvantage of the science side, for the head boy had just got a major scholarship at Trinity College, Cambridge, in physics. This is one form of equality on the right lines. 'Parity of esteem', an ideal usually in England applied only to the relations of the Secondary Grammar and the Secondary Modern schools, is just as important and easier to achieve in the relations between the Secondary Grammar (County) Schools and the public schools.

The idea that education is a commodity dies hard. There are still people who believe that all that is needed in education is application. Something of this idea is associated with the days when labour too was a commodity. It is not surprising that when in England the opportunity of education was deliberately kept from the working classes they in turn should feel that education, like other good things of life, was not being shared out properly. William Lovett, the Chartist, in 1837 denounced the upper classes for looking on education as 'a boon to be sparingly conferred upon the multitude', instead of being, as he said, 'a RIGHT, a right derivable from society itself',[1] Education along one sort of class line was bound to create a demand along another sort of class line. It is this commodity theory that is evident in Communist countries but it is not unknown even in countries of free enterprise such as the United States. I also once found the commodity theory in full working order in an entirely African school in Nigeria. I asked the African headmaster what subject was the most popular in his school. Without hesitation he replied 'Latin'. When I asked why, he said: 'Latin is what you have in your English schools, therefore we want it here also.' There was no other reason.

[1] *Life and Struggles of William Lovett in his Pursuit of Bread, Knowledge and Freedom* (1876), reprinted 1920, with a preface by R. H. Tawney, vol. 1, p. 142.

Education works upon differences and therefore any specific type of education must take into account the pupil's ability to profit by it and make it his own. This is the only genuine standard, and yet many others are often found. It has been assumed, for instance, that in craft subjects girls should do cookery just because they are girls and boys should do carpentry just because they are boys. But the division of interest does not necessarily follow sex lines at all. One well-known boarding school for girls has carpentry as one of its subjects, and there are technical schools which teach cookery to boys. By the same token there is no genuine hierarchy of subjects. It is not 'better' to do classics or mathematics than to do domestic science or physical education. Classics is 'best' for those who have a particular aptitude for classics and physical education is 'best' for those who can do it well, and in the last resort the 'bests' are all equal. The principle that makes one subject more valuable than another depends upon the window it opens in a pupil's mind and upon the landscape that is revealed by it. This, of course, is to put into plain language what Spearman meant by arranging subjects according to the '*G*' or general factor that they possess over against the '*S*' or specific training that they give. But this is only half the story, for these capacities are not in the subjects themselves but in the subjects as mediated to the pupil through the teacher's own attitude. Classics can be taught as a dull matter of looking up the meanings of words in a dictionary, while mathematics can be so taught as to open one's eyes to the wonders of creation, although the general opinion might be otherwise. Equality in education, therefore, involves the teacher's method and the teacher's personality as well as the subject and the pupil's capacity and the pupil's interest.

It is also worth noticing that there is a necessary element of compulsion in education for the very profound reason that appreciation of education comes *after* education. It cannot be left to the pupil alone to decide what he will and will not do. The weakness of many so-called progressive schools is that they allow the pupil to choose his own lines at the particular time and place where he happens to be now, and without first giving him the instruments by which he is to make a choice. How many children if left entirely to their own devices would choose English grammar or algebra as desirable matters with which to occupy themselves? Some no doubt would do so, but it is not possible to tell until they have started. There must therefore be compulsion somewhere, and the reason why in later years there is more and more specialization is not only because it is impossible to study thoroughly more than a limited section of knowledge but also because as a result of earlier compulsion a variety of choices have been spread before the pupil and he has learned to choose. Thus paradoxically liberty comes through compulsion just as equality, also paradoxically, comes through the manipulation of differences.

From this there follows a very important principle which has repercussions all over the world, for it is vitally concerned with political action. The principle is that education is needed in order to reveal to a man and to his neighbours what manner of man he is. In other words, we do not first decide that a person has such and such abilities and interests and then give him the education best suited to them; the education is needed first in order to discover what are those abilities and interests. This is a consideration which cuts across all barriers of sex, race, colour, class, creed or nation.

## 7 ILLUSTRATIONS FROM SOCIAL CLASS, RACE AND SEX

Let us take three illustrations, each involving a particular kind of equality.

First with regard to class equality. Up to the end of the nineteenth century Disraeli's theory of the two nations domiciled in the same country of England was a correct diagnosis. In a little village café in Somerset I once came across an old number of the *Illustrated London News* which I found most interesting. The date was 1855 and the period that of the Crimean War. The War Office had apparently just discovered that it was necessary to dig trenches out on the battlefield. This was considered to be work for navvies and not for the troops and so a consignment of navvies was ordered to the Crimea and Lord Adolphus Fitzclarence went down to Portsmouth to see them off. He made a speech to them which could not have been different had it been made to a boat-load of strange animals. There was no recognition that these were men, let alone Englishmen. The class distinction had become almost racial!

It was often asked what sort of education should be given to working men such as these. For years it was assumed that there was such a thing as the working-class mind, which was quite different from the mind of other people and therefore it needed a special type of education. It was a president of the Royal Society who declared in Parliament in 1807:

> However specious in theory the project might be of giving education to the labouring classes of the poor it would in effect be found to be prejudicial to their morals and happiness: it would teach them to despise their lot in life instead of making them good servants in agriculture and other laborious employments to which their rank in society had destined them.[1]

The same point of view was expressed by writers in *Blackwood's Magazine*: 'the only education fit for poor people is a religious one, which renders them patient, humble and moral'.[2] This feeling runs through the Newcastle Commission Report of 1861, and was one cause of the opposition to the Education Act of 1870.

Education, however, was provided or at any rate subsidized in minute quantities by the State; but after a few years there came to light another characteristic of education. It was discovered that it cannot be stopped. The appreciation of a little education leads to the demand for more and better. Elementary schools added to their numbers older children who wished to go further and finally the State had to come in and start a system of secondary education. It was at this point that class distinction was on trial. Should the children of working men be given an education 'fitted' for working men or should they have a type of education similar to that of the public schools? In other words, was secondary educa-

[1] Speech by Davies Giddy, in de Montmorency, *State Intervention in English Education* (1902), pp. 222–3.

[2] H. Holman, *English National Education* (1898), p. 59.

tion to be an extension of elementary education or was it to be a different kind of thing altogether? The secretary of the Board of Education, Sir Robert Morant, decided on the second. If it was ever to be demonstrated that the children of working men had brains as good as the children of the upper classes they must be able to vindicate that on the upper classes' own ground. And this meant that they must have the same type of education. Very many no doubt would fall by the wayside, and for them such education would have been proved to be unsuitable, but they would at any rate have had the chance to prove themselves. But a few, perhaps only a very few to begin with, would have shown to the world that ability did not run along class lines and that if there were any village Miltons who remained mute and inglorious it was a slur on the community that had muzzled them. Differences remained, but as usual equality was something to be demonstrated, not claimed.

The same principle operates, secondly, in regard to race differences. It has been offered as the justification of the South African policy of 'apartheid' that the African is a different kind of human being from the white man and therefore needs to be developed 'along his own lines'. There is a specious reasonableness about this position, for everybody really needs to be developed along his own lines and it is the task of education to assist in that process. But the South African assumption is that it is known *in advance* what those lines are, that it is for the whites to inform the blacks what those lines are, and that the determining line of division is by colour and race. All this of course is flatly against the proved principle that it is impossible to know beforehand what a person's abilities and interests are, and that it is only education that will reveal them. But in this argument the whole of the black people of South Africa and indeed of the world are comprehended under one classification. The ablest black compared with the stupidest white is classified not according to his ability but according to the colour of his skin—a completely irrelevant factor in education.

When I was last in Mafeking a very interesting situation had arisen in the local hospital. Two white men suffering from angina had besought a local specialist on heart disease to accept them as patients. He happened to be an African but he was also a doctor of medicine of the University of Glasgow. He was unwilling to take them on as they were hospital cases. However, he gave in eventually and sent them both into hospital. When he went in next day to see them all the white nurses walked out. They were afterwards congratulated by Nationalist members of Parliament on the fine stand they had taken for white civilization! The Hospital Committee met and passed a minute banning the doctor from the hospital. All the nurses came back. Then the South African Medical Association met and banned the hospital for preventing a fully qualified doctor from carrying out his professional duties. Accordingly if the Committee let the doctor in they got no nurses and if they kept him out they got no doctors! This Gilbertian situation could have arisen only in a country where colour was confused with mental qualities with which it has really nothing to do.

As an ironical comment on this it is interesting to notice that a bill was introduced into the South African Parliament on 17 April 1957 which provided that anyone who caused a white nurse to be placed under the control or supervision of anyone who was not white in any hospital or similar institution would be guilty of an offence and liable on conviction to a fine not exceeding £200.

As far back as 1853 the report of an education commission in Natal laid down 'agricultural education of an elementary type for the Natives' (this presumably included potential doctors, clergymen, lawyers and professors) and furthermore that 'the Kaffirs should be taught to respect the white man and realise their own immense inferiority'.[1] This was over a hundred years ago, but for many people the attitude has not changed. We might well ask how it would ever have been possible for anybody to know that this particular African that I have mentioned had it in him to be one of the leading heart specialists in the Union if he had been given only an agricultural education?

[1] E. H. Brookes, *A History of Native Policy in South Africa* (1927), p. 55.

The South African reply to this is interesting. It is held that there is to be no attempt to prevent the African having education, even the most specialized medical education, so long as he gets it among black people and carries on his profession among black people only. That is what 'apartheid' really means. It is not keeping the African down: it is simply preventing him from mixing with the whites.

The difficulty here is indicated by the story of the doctor. There was a white doctor in Mafeking at the same time as Dr Molema but he was an ordinary general practitioner with none of the specialized knowledge that these cases needed. Specialized ability does not follow racial lines and its sphere of activity is determined by the needs that have to be met rather than by such an absurd test as colour or race. The whole South African position is a savage attack on equality—equality of any kind—social, educational, economic and even religious—and its insincerity is seen even more in its attitude to the whites than in its attitude to the blacks. 'Apartheid' is held to be necessary to safeguard white civilization. The white students of the University of Witwatersrand do not think so, nor do the Cape Town tramway authorities, nor does the white Bishop of Johannesburg, nor do thousands of other white people. But as the Government possesses the physical instruments of power these people are being coerced into acting against their consciences, because what is opposed to them is not reasoned argument but naked force.

My third example of the way in which education cuts across barriers is taken from the history of women's education in Cambridge University.

'The will of God', says Barbara Stephen in her life of Emily Davies, 'and the "laws of Nature" were constantly and complacently quoted as the foundation on which the submission of women was based, and it was against this tremendous opposition that the pioneers of women's education carried on their work.' In Cambridge there were ultimately set up two colleges—Newnham, in the heart of the town in order that the girls might attend lectures without taking examinations, and Girton, two miles out, where the girls took the university examinations but were not concerned about university lectures. Later both colleges attended lectures and both took the examinations, but in neither case were the women given degrees. At a certain point, however, the Cambridge University authorities, acting on the same principle of 'apartheid' which later actuated the South African Nationalists, offered to set up what would have been in effect a parallel University of Cambridge for the women. They would have their own lectures, their own examinations and their own degrees. Miss Clough of Newnham was inclined to accept this as the victory for which she had been fighting, but Miss Davies of Girton would not look at it. And in rejecting it she laid down a principle which is of universal application. 'If', she said in effect, 'you have differentiation before you have equality you will never get equality.' This is profoundly true. How could it ever be held that women's brains are as good as men's if they were denied all opportunity of competing with men? Differentiation at that stage would have meant a stereotyping of inequality. This principle held good with working men's education, the education of Africans and the education of women.

It should be noted in passing what a tremendous strain this lays upon the pioneers. The men at Cambridge had behind them the heritage of several centuries of higher education which stood them in good stead when they sought entrance to the universities. The girls' schools had just been started, there were few of them, and the standard was not nearly as high as that of the boys' schools. University education as it was at that time was therefore in a sense most unsuitable for the girls. Nevertheless they had to suffer all those handicaps in order to have the chance of beating the men on their own ground. And when in 1890 the last citadel was stormed and in the mathematical tripos a woman was ranked above the Senior Wrangler, the battle was won. Again, equality had to be a matter of demonstration rather than the assertion of a claim. It is precisely that kind of demonstration that the South African Government is trying at all costs to prevent.

## 8 THE CONTROL OF EDUCATION

Whose business is it to provide and control or direct education? The Roman Catholic point of view has always been that education is a function of the Church. The American point of view is that it is the function of the State. A Dean of Bristol in 1861 seemed to think it was the business of the employer. In his evidence before the Newcastle Commission he said: 'It is only to attempt the task of Mrs Partington over again to set ourselves to stem back the demands of the labour market.' In South Africa the Government is the sole authority for education, for even a white school where criticism of the Government is allowed may be closed on grounds of 'sedition'. In Russia the Communists alone are allowed to educate.

It is clear that the claims made for a good many of these authorities are claims not on behalf of education but of propaganda. This is to say, they are concerned not with the pupil but with themselves. They are claims that their own views may be heard to the exclusion of every other, and an insistence that their own views must be accepted. Right or wrong have no meaning in such a context. The sole issue is conformity or non-conformity. This is the crude way of producing equality of opinion, not by accepting differences but by ignoring them. It is the negation of both liberty and equality, and is out of place in a free society.

The question, however, of the Church's place in education is a very vital one, for it brings in the questions of liberty and of equality and of the relation between them. It must be remembered that in the West the Church was for centuries the leading and sometimes the only educator. It did, moreover, ignore class distinctions and at times gave ability its opportunity. It is interesting to notice how many high-ranking officers in Church and State in the Middle Ages came from very humble homes. The old jingle about Cardinal Wolsey declared him to have been 'begot by butchers' but nevertheless allowed that he was 'by bishops bred'. The case for the continuance of control of education by the Church is often urged on the ground that it has always had it and that it has on the whole done a good job of work in it. If, however, we have arrived at the stage where education is a civil right it must be the concern of the community as a whole. And the community as a whole must maintain its right against any other agency, the Church, the employers or even the parents. Article 26 in the United Nations' Declaration of Human Rights declares that 'parents have a prior right to choose the kind of education that shall be given to their children'. On the assumption that the parents are not really competent to decide between different 'kinds' of education this right in Roman Catholic countries is taken over by the Church, presumably as acting for the parents, and the slogan 'the rights of parents' has no force. Have parents the right in such countries to bring up their children as Communists or atheists? If we believe in the rights of parents we cannot deny them just because we disapprove of some particular exercise of those rights. Society comprises all sorts and conditions of men, and rights that are claimed by one section cannot very well be denied to another. There cannot be incorporated into the relations of Church and State a 'most favoured denomination' clause as, in certain political treaties, one is inserted on behalf of a 'most favoured nation'.

If education is the great agency for producing equality while accepting differences, it might seem that sectional control of education is the surest way to confirm inequality. It is here, however, that the distinction already made between the Church as an institution and the Church as the total sum of professing Christians may be useful. The Church as an institution in a free society does not enter into education simply as a matter of right. We all like to have our own way, and Christians have not been backward in exhibiting this common characteristic. But an organized society such as a denomination cannot take out of the hands of another organized society, the community as a whole, responsibility which is the concern of the community as a whole. Nevertheless the tone and spirit and aim of education are of as vital importance to the Church in a general sense as to the State also in a general sense. It has been shown in another context that ownership is not in the least necessary to appreciation or influence.[1] Ownership in matters of education can belong only to institutions, and private institutions like private persons are not competent to handle the children of an entire community. The Church, however, in this more general sense, while it cannot own the agencies of education, can most certainly influence them, and probably with more effect without ownership than with it. The Church in this sense, even in a country only nominally Christian, can show concern for excellence—both in the subjects taught and in the way of teaching them. After all, the Church's primary task is with persons rather than property and it should aim by its influence on persons to make the road easier for the passage of moral ideas and still more to make possible a dispassionate yet committed attitude to life and spiritual values. Propaganda is not concerned with persons but with the institution, and while the road is longer and more difficult through education it leads in the end to a genuine equality of appreciation with scope for differences. In our concern for equality we are not forgetting liberty. Parents have the rights in these matters as well as churches or employers or the community. But the rights of parents as of the other parties in the situation should be exercised only in the direction of excellence, and it is by this means rather than by sectarian or social or other prejudices that the parent will help to raise the standard of education and ought to be allowed to do so. The situation no doubt bristles with difficulties and like every other human situation it can be properly met only by good will. To attempt to legislate for sectional interests, particularly if they are institutional or vested interests, is one sure way of denying liberty to those most concerned, namely the children.

[1] Above, p. 121.

CHAPTER XI

# FRATERNITY

## I THE MIRAGE OF FRATERNITY

John Addington Symonds in a famous hymn put into words what most men have in their heart of hearts desired concerning society, and we might take two of its verses as a text.

> These things shall be: a loftier race
> Than e'er the world hath known shall rise,
> With flame of freedom in their souls
> And light of knowledge in their eyes.
>
> Nation with nation, land with land,
> Inarmed shall live as comrades free;
> In every heart and brain shall throb
> The pulse of one fraternity.

Dr Rendel Harris used to refer to this as the 'eugenic hymn'. It is not addressed to any deity. It is simply the expression of a wish and the affirmation of a hope. Nevertheless in assemblies of starry-eyed business-men and of ethical societies it gives an uplift to the spirit and makes goodness and altruism for a moment passionately desirable. For this is the land of heart's desire—no more war, no cut-throat competition, no oppression, no crime, every man pulling his weight and serving his fellows in the brotherhood of man and the federation of the world.

Yet the situation as we find it is completely different. If anyone wished to take seriously the epilogue to Thomas Hardy's *Tess of the d'Urbervilles*—that the President of the Immortals had been simply having a game with Tess as with all other creatures here below—he could hardly get better confirmation of it than the persistence of this mirage of fraternity, the reality of which as persistently eludes our grasp. Why is this idea so ineffective in the practical affairs of life? What is the cause of this frustration? Is it the Church's fault? Is it the fault of the State? Is capitalism the real stumbling block or is it the intransigence of labour? The Communists put it down to the *bourgeoisie*, the Nazis blamed the Jews. Some people think there is more likelihood of the free society arriving across the Atlantic and so they are on their way out to meet it, while a few isolated individuals think they will find it in India. In all this welter of suggestions and desires and plans there seems to be only one common factor and that is the heart of man. So many good social intentions come to shipwreck sooner or later on the strong rock of human frailty, and yet the marvellous thing is that men swim ashore and begin at once to refit the vessel for another voyage. If hopes were dupes at any rate fears may be liars and it is worth trying just once more.

In this unexpected and rather extraordinary human situation, Church and State have taken different lines. From the political and economic point of view fraternity is the end of the road. This is the goal which we all seek or at any rate which each of us expects the other man to seek. This is why we are organized in groups and communities, why we study to improve the relationship between classes and races and nations, why we pore over blue-books and blue-prints, why we have elections and changes of government, and indeed why we act at all on the economic and political plane. It will be a very long road, no doubt, but this is the direction in which we are going. Unfortunately it is the commonest thing in the world for men to fall out by the way, and in the name of fraternity to commit as many crimes as in the name of liberty. 'Big Brother' somehow suggests the very reverse of brotherhood.

The Christian view is different. The brotherhood of man follows at once from the fatherhood of God. Fraternity is thus not a goal but a present fact, just as the fatherhood of God is a present fact, something to be acted upon here and now. It is with this that we begin here and now to construct a new world, and put into operation fraternity without tarrying for any. The kingdom of heaven is not Utopia: it is within us and seeking all the time an outward expression. The early Christians were not prisoners of hope: they were men who had been made free and at once began to treat other men as free. The fraternity of the early Church was a description of the way in which they lived and not simply a piece of propaganda for the future, and the Sermon on the Mount is an illustration of how you could live the life of brotherhood in the conditions in Palestine in the first century. We have to provide our own illustrations of how it can be done in Britain and America in the twentieth century.

There are two considerations which make possible this attitude of brotherhood. One, obviously, is recognition of the common fatherhood and the other is personal commitment to Christ. This is not to say that there are no people who act by these ideals except those who are committed to this loyalty. This is certainly not true, but unless there was a core of committed people *somewhere* the idea of Christian brotherhood would simply be lost among the other Utopias and come to nothing. But there has to be in each generation an infusion of new blood into the ranks of the committed in order to keep alive not so much the belief in fraternity as its day-to-day practice.

In the second place, the recognition of the common fatherhood is, as we have seen, the very basis of a Christian structure of politics. It gives the family pattern for human relationships. It is within this circle that there is liberty with authority and equality with difference. It is here that the ideals present in both Church and State come together, and it is this which is intended to be the regulative principle of both of them.

What then are the factors which make this family relationship what it is? It is necessary to consider this before we can face the greatest obstacle to human brotherhood, wars and rumours of wars.

## 2 THE FAMILY AS A PATTERN FOR POLITICS

The family is the oldest institution in the world, and yet it is not strictly an institution at all. It is a biological fact and its concern is with the continuance and the education of the race. It has within it the two chief divisions of mankind—male and female, youth and age—divisions which if opposed to one another can be fatal to human happiness, but which if wisely appreciated can result in such concord as can never be produced by mere uniformity. Tension is an inevitable factor in all human relationships; it is not to be avoided but to be resolved. The progress of mankind can be described as a movement from a situation in which tension causes war to a situation in which tension is a major cause of peace. The present attitude of the nations of the world, armed to the teeth against one another, is an indication of how far we are from accepting human brotherhood. The continuance of the family, on the other hand, is an indication of the possibility of the resolution of tension and the creation of happiness. And in certain ways, economic and political as well as domestic, the family is the pattern of human relationships. Although it is a biological group, something that we share with the higher animals, it has always had about it this ethical quality, and the fact that this involuntary natural association should have such a quality suggests that morality instead of being a convention of a particular society is a primal attribute of human nature. While there are no doubt thousands of families in which tension leads to disruption, the balance must be the other way, otherwise the family would have disappeared long ago.

The tensions within the family are of several kinds and the relationship between them is interesting. The first is that between male and female, and at the beginning it is that between husband and wife. The idea of tension, of course, is quite other than that of disagreement. Tension is there even when there is a state of complete harmony. A spinning top spins in silence because there is a perfect balance of all the forces playing upon it. It is only as it runs down that the forces begin to act against one another and it begins to make a noise. There is a permanent difference between one person and another, a difference which is not abolished even when these two are husband and wife. There is added to this distinction the further distinction of difference between the sexes. And the fact that love is the basis of the association has the curious ambivalent effect of increasing the sense of difference at the same time as it increases the sense of oneness. Thus difference—which, after all, means only a recognition that each person is a unique creation and has his own life to live—can provide a firmer ground for fellowship than exact conformity. It is this truth which is ignored by every totalitarian regime because its principle of association is mechanical and quantitative and quite unlike the relationship within a family.

These two lines of tension, therefore—person and person, man and woman—are present at the very outset. It is worthy of note that when these come together to form a permanent association a number of other considerations at once come into view. Anthropologists have shown that the further you go back in human society the more strict and complicated are the regulations that hedge round this relationship. Promiscuity is a feature of the so-called advanced societies rather than of the primitive. It is as though the single relationship of man and woman, apart from children, has in itself a certain completeness, and that the resolving of this particular tension is a preliminary requirement before it becomes complicated by the arrival of children. It may be that this is the ultimate reason behind what is called an engagement or a betrothal, which in some societies is taken much more seriously than in the countries of the West.

This view, of course, is not quite in accord with the Book of Common Prayer where the first object of marriage is stated to be the procreation of children, the second the avoidance of sin, and only the third is for mutual society. On the other hand it is somewhat embarrassing to find that it is in accordance with a judgement of the Lord Chancellor in an important divorce case in 1947.

The couple concerned married on the understanding that they were not to have any children. As time went on, however, the husband wanted to have a family, but his wife clung to the original agreement. For ten years the husband tried to persuade her otherwise but without success. He therefore petitioned for the marriage to be annulled. The case came before various courts and the appeal was finally dismissed by the House of Lords. In giving his judgement,

the Lord Chancellor said that the insistence on the procreation of children as one of the principal ends, if not the principal end of marriage, required examination. It was indisputable that the institution of marriage generally was not necessary for the procreation of children, nor did it appear to be a principal end of marriage as understood in Christendom, which as Lord Penzance said in *Hyde* v. *Hyde* (1866) 'may for this purpose be defined as the voluntary union for life of one man and one woman, to the exclusion of all others'.

As regards the phraseology of the marriage service in the Prayer Book that House in *Weatherley* v. *Weatherley* (63 The Times L.R. 209 (1947)) pointed out the dangers of too strict a reliance on those words. In any view of Christian marriage the essence of the matter, as it seemed to him, was that the children, if there were any, should be born into a family, as that word was understood in Christendom generally, and in the case of marriage between spouses of a particular faith that they should be brought up and nurtured in that faith. But that was not the same thing as saying that a marriage was not consummated unless children were procreated or that the procreation of children was the principal end of marriage.[1]

This judgement led to considerable correspondence. One letter pointed out that marriage was a status rather than a contract, and that a petition for nullity is not an attempt to rescind the contract but 'an attempt to get judicial recognition of the fact that the status of husband and wife has never existed between the parties'. This position, of course, is flatly against the Lord Chancellor's judgement. So also is the position indicated in another letter to the effect that in the teaching of 'the Western or Catholic' church a marriage does not become indissoluble until it has been consummated by physical intercourse, and until then a marriage can for sufficient reason be dissolved.

This obsession with the physical side of marriage, with the procreation of children and with the prevention of fornication, has bedevilled all discussion that has ever taken place in Christendom concerning the nature of marriage and the rightness or wrongness of divorce. It has left out of account the spiritual value

[1] *The Times*, 18 December 1947, L.R., Baxter *v*. Baxter.

that exists or can exist in the life-long association of two persons whether they have children or not, and it permits religious people to give no thought at all to homes which are a hell upon earth but to protest at once if there is any attempt to end such a situation between two persons whom it is alleged that God has joined together. There is probably more cant talked—on both sides—on this marriage question than on any other source of conflict between Church and State. 'Indissolubility' and 'whom God hath joined' are at times merely stock phrases used on one side like 'mental cruelty' and 'incompatibility' on the other.

## 3 BIBLICAL VIEW OF MARRIAGE AND DIVORCE

As this is the point at which Church and State come most violently into conflict we must spend a little time sorting out the issues.

The emphasis on the physical side of marriage goes even further than the question of physical intercourse. It has been assumed, for instance, that the marriage rite itself *ex opere operato* works a magical change in the bodies of the persons concerned. So much is this the case that if one partner dies and the survivor marries the deceased wife's sister or the deceased husband's brother he or she is guilty of incest. This fear of incest has a very long history, far farther back than Christian times, and it is the cause of the extraordinarily complicated 'tables of affinity' that are respected by every savage tribe. In the Christian dispensation, however, it is strengthened by the crudely literal application of a text in Genesis which is quoted in two places in the Gospels—'they shall be one flesh'. The text is part of the story of the creation of woman out of the body of man and states that because man and woman in the beginning were literally one flesh *therefore* a man cleaves to his wife, 'the attachment between them becoming greater and the union closer even than that between parent and child. Marriage—and moreover monogamic marriage—is thus explained as the direct consequence of a relation established by the Creator.[1]

The text in Genesis, however, might have been considered as

[1] S. R. Driver, *The Book of Genesis*, *sub* ii. 21–4.

merely part of the folk-lore of the Old Testament, were it not for the fact that it is quoted by Our Lord and thereby apparently becomes regulative of Christian thinking on this question. Whenever isolated texts are used to substantiate a position capable of being taken up for other reasons, we do well to be cautious.[1] The texts in this case are Matthew v. 32 and xix. 9; Mark x. 4–12; Luke xvi. 18; Romans vii. 3; I Corinthians vii. 10, 11. They are for the most part concerned with marriage as much as with divorce and it would appear that the possibility or impossibility, the rightness or wrongness of divorce, is altogether dependent on what is our view of marriage. The two go together, yet they are not always taken together. Take for instance the phrase 'whom God hath joined'. What exactly does it mean? The Roman Church, which does not acknowledge divorce, would justify its position on the Scriptural ground that those whom God hath joined should not by man be put asunder. But it is reasonable to ask if *God* has joined two people who go to the registrar's office to get married. Presumably, on the Roman position, he must have done, otherwise there would be no objection on these grounds to divorce. And how does the 'joining' take place? Is it done by the pronunciation of certain words? Or is it done by the act of signing the register afterwards?

These are questions which very naturally arise from a literal acceptance of these texts which is all too common. But if we accept the historical method of exegesis and seek to interpret the New Testament in the light and in the context of the contemporary situation, a far more radical treatment is needed. We need first of all to acquaint ourselves with the position of women in those days, with the Old Testament teaching on this matter, with the discussions that went on between the rival Rabbinical schools of Hillel and Shamnai, and, above all, with the general attitude of Jesus to all human questions.

What then is the situation? Jesus' teaching about marriage is stated to have arisen in response to an approach by the Pharisees

[1] E.g. the Roman Catholic claims based on Matthew xvi. 18, 19 and xviii. 18, and the South African doctrine of *apartheid* justified by appeal to Genesis ix. 25.

'tempting him'. On two other such occasions when the Pharisees tempt him he gives oracular replies: 'Render therefore unto Caesar the things which be Caesar's' and 'When they shall rise from the dead, they neither marry, nor are given in marriage; but are as the angels which are in heaven'—in each case an *argumentum ad hominem* the interpretation of which would not be lost on his contemporary hearers. In another place where he was criticized—when the woman anointed him with the ointment—he gave a similar type of reply, 'Ye have the poor with you always, and whensoever ye will ye may do them good'. 'Tempting him' in all these cases implied the attempt to put him in a dilemma where the hardness of the law was set over against his well-known concern for people. In this matter of marriage, however, the reverse seems to be the case. It is an attempt to contrast the slackness of the law with Jesus' regard for standards, and apparently to put him into a position where regard for people took second place to regard for the law.

What sort of reply therefore did the Pharisees expect to receive when they emphasized the Mosaic permission of divorce? And in his reply whom had Jesus in mind to rebuke and whom to protect? It will be noted that ancient law in these matters, not excluding the Old Testament, was heavily weighted on the side of the man. These texts on divorce are all concerned in the main with the man's point of view and with the putting away of the woman. It was strictly against the law for a woman to put away her husband, and Josephus strongly condemns the courtesans Salome and Herodias for so doing.[1] Women on the whole had a very poor treatment in these matters. Even the Mosaic law by requiring a 'bill of divorcement', which was intended to stay proceedings and give the man time to think again, put no restraint on his conduct towards his wife. The Rabbis allowed all kinds of ridiculous grounds for divorce, such as breaking a vow, appearing in public with dishevelled hair, or burning the husband's dinner![2]

It is this attitude that Jesus rebukes in his reply. He protects the

[1] *Antiquities*, XV, 7, 10; XVIII, 5, 4.

[2] *The Mishnah*, Gittin. (Danby's edition, 1933, p. 321.)

wife by putting a heavy obligation on the husband. He emphasizes the seriousness of the married state for the man, since as things stood in his time it was the woman on whom were laid the heavier obligations. This means, therefore, that in the mind of Jesus the marriage relationship was determined neither by cast-iron rule nor by indiscriminate licence. It is a reminder that there are many factors in the situation, and that the most important of them is a regard for the people concerned.

It is notable that none of this teaching appears in the Fourth Gospel. Instead, we have the story of the woman taken in adultery, an incident in which Jesus deliberately by-passes the Mosaic law in favour, in this case, not of a more stringent regulation but of a more compassionate attitude. But the story is once more introduced as a reply to the Pharisees 'tempting him' and there is again the reference to Moses. Throughout the Gospels the leading theme in relation to persons is compassion. In incident after incident this is the principle on which Jesus deals with people. To lay down a rigid rule was never his way. In his teaching about God the keynote is not power nor sovereignty but fatherhood and compassion.

Why then does the teaching about divorce seem to differ altogether from his usual attitude that the Sabbath was made for man and not man for the Sabbath? Why is a stricter rule laid down which would appear to be at variance with Jesus' general position?

The answer is that it is not at variance but in harmony. The person on whom he had compassion here was the divorced woman. The law of Moses was what it was because of the 'hardness of [men's] hearts'—because it did not seem possible to get them to adopt a humane standard in relation to their fellows. In the matter of revenge it compromised with man's revengeful nature by limiting it to an eye for an eye and a tooth for a tooth instead of pursuing the wrong-doer to the death. But Jesus put in place of that rule a new commandment, that men should love their enemies. Similarly the Mosaic allowance of a bill of divorcement was an attempt to help the wife a little by making the husband take time to consider. But Jesus goes further and protects the wife by insisting that the husband should recognize from the start that marriage was a solemn covenant intended to be lifelong. It was God who brought them together, and it was therefore unjust for a man to treat his wife as an object to be thrown aside like an old glove when he had got tired of her.

The intransigence of the Church in interpreting this teaching as an inflexible rule automatically penalizing everybody concerned in a divorce is so alien to the spirit of the Master as to amount to a betrayal. It has also obliged the State to step in to mitigate ecclesiastical harshness. The State has to consider all the factors in the situation even if the Church continues to look at only some of them. The real evil of indiscriminate divorce, the easy plea of 'mental cruelty' or 'incompatibility', is not that it breaks a supposed rigid rule of God, but that it represents a shockingly callous view of human personality.

It cannot be too strongly emphasized that Biblical contexts and exegesis are as important as texts, and indeed texts without contexts can be grossly misleading. Their only advantage is as a time-saving device to the man who is either too ignorant or too lazy to discover what they really mean. A typical example of this sort of thing was reported in the *Daily Mail* of Monday, 26 October 1953. It appeared that a new vicar had been appointed to a rural parish in Devon. There he discovered that the squire of the parish, the present head of an old family which had worshipped there for five hundred years, had twenty-five years before been the innocent party in a divorce suit. The squire had married again and all his five children had been baptized in the parish church. Nevertheless the vicar took upon himself to ban the squire from Communion, and he was reported as having said: 'It matters not that he was the innocent party in the divorce. Christ's teaching on that particular subject is detailed in the tenth chapter of St Mark and no priest can ignore it. I have nothing against him as a man but if he should approach my [*sic*] altar I should refuse him Communion and he has been told so.'

Twenty-five years is a long time, even longer than the sentence of a criminal sentenced 'for life'. But apparently there is no way even after a quarter of a century whereby this man can be received at the Lord's table. The vicar, it should be noticed, chose to base his position on this single text in Mark, ignoring Matthew where in two places there is added the saving clause 'save for fornication'. Jesus' attitude is even more clearly seen in the story of the woman taken in adultery, an attitude of which the vicar would apparently have disapproved.

I have spent some time in trying to elucidate the New Testament idea of brotherhood because it is through misinterpretation at this point that all other ideas of brotherhood go wrong. First of all it is concerned with God and a conviction that, as God is the father of all men, all men are not intended to become but actually *are* brothers. Every war therefore is a civil war, every act of oppression is an offence against the family. Just as in the law of the land an offence against a person is not a private affair but is a breach of the King's peace, so an offence against a member of the human family is a breach of God's peace. Then secondly, the relationships of persons within the family are determined not by a rigid code but by those ties which, in Burke's words, 'though light as air are as strong as links of iron'—namely love, sympathy, compassion, unselfishness and appreciation of differences. These intangible, imponderable associations are more effective because more acceptable than any third-party authority. It is through the atheism of disbelief in the strength of these qualities and the refusal first to create them and then to rely upon them that marriage is hedged in by external rules, that pacts and treaties are believed to be more effective between nations than good will, and that when the rules are ignored or the treaties broken the relationships dissolve at once into chaos. If the family is, as I believe it to be, the pattern of all human association and of the relation between God and man as the New Testament clearly indicates, then the sanctions must be those of love and not of regulations. God does not join people together by the utterance of certain words, no matter how solemnly pronounced. The theory that he does goes back to the Roman law of contract, and the sanctions imposed by the Church for breach of that contract go back to the same source. Thirdly, therefore, if the family idea is neglected and replaced by a rigid code easy to apply, the situation becomes one of immense spiritual danger to the people who have the power to apply it. If Acton's dictum is true that all power tends to corrupt and absolute power to corrupt absolutely, there is no more certain cause of corruption than that which places in the hands of men an instrument of spiritual tyranny over the lives of other men.

## 4 CONSCIENCE AND THE COMMUNITY

In the case of the Devonshire vicar it may be a question to decide whether his position was a genuine theological one or whether he was the victim of his own peculiar ideology. A somewhat similar case arose a year or two ago in the case of a Methodist minister. It was reported in the papers that a certain Methodist church in the Midlands had a keen choirmaster, a faithful member of the church. He had a 'flutter' on the football pools and he won £700. For this offence, which apparently had not been declared to be an offence until it took place, the minister made him resign all his offices in the church. The man was naturally very much upset, and when later he committed suicide the tragedy was commonly ascribed to this harsh judgement. No doubt there were facts in the case that were not reported, but there was here enough evidence to show a lamentable failure of Christian charity on the part of somebody.

These two cases indicate how tenuous is the bond of fraternity when an ideology gets in the way. And I believe that in both cases it was due to an ideology rather than to any theological argument that these men acted as they did. The point at which genuine religious considerations harden into an ideology is when they are cut off from the mind of Christ and they become esteemed for their own logical completeness. Any theology which is Christian must have about it a certain elasticity, for it is concerned with that most sensitive of God's creations—human life, both in itself and in its relation to the living God. Clearly this cannot be contained in a hard and rigid casing. At all times allowance must be made for the unexpected, since neither God nor man can be fully known by any human being. Nothing, for instance, could have been more unexpected than Christ's treatment of the woman taken in adultery. Both the law and the fact were beyond question and there seemed no way of getting out of either. But the desires of the accusers were to the mind of Jesus quite invalid, for these men were treating the case from the wrong end. They were concerned with the law of Moses, clear, logical, complete, but utterly unsympathetic. Jesus views the matter from the human end and makes allowances of one sort for the woman but also of another sort for her accusers. The justice of God, as we have already seen,[1] is compounded with what we call mercy, and Jesus treated the woman from the standpoint of justice rather than from that of law. That is to say, he applied a flexible standard to the situation rather than one that was rigid and unhuman. Yet the law of Moses was not set aside, and the argument of the accusers was fully accepted, but they were put into the position of having themselves to decide the case from the standpoint of Jesus and not in accordance with their own ideology.

It may well be asked whether a failure in Christian charity is not a greater reason for banning a man from Communion or from church membership than the reasons advanced in these two cases which we have just considered.

The relevance of this discussion to our main subject lies in the fact that religious reasons are often adduced in an issue of Church and State when the real case that is being urged (from either side) is that of an ideological position. Indeed fraternity may itself be an ideology and may be pressed solely with an urge for completeness, to round off, as it were, a position which appears to be anything but fraternal. The 'Big Brother' motif, and the classless society, have their origin not in any warm-hearted regard for the other person but in a desire, indeed a lust, to squeeze him into a pre-arranged pattern. It is because of this defect of approach that there seems no likelihood of Russia of its own will delivering up its German prisoners or setting free the countries that groan under

[1] Above, pp. 39 f.

its yoke. The Russian Communist shares with the primitive savage a total inability to enter into the feelings of other men and to be moved by them. But this is a characteristic of ideologists everywhere, even in Britain.[1]

We need, therefore, to make ourselves sure that the attitude of resistance to a government is based on a genuine appeal to conscience and not to an ideology. During World War I, before the case of the conscientious objector had been fully understood, a very mixed crowd found themselves in prison for the same overt attitudes but for vastly different reasons. In the jail at Wakefield the conscientious objectors discovered that they fell into two classes—those who were prepared to assist a sympathetic governor and staff to carry out their unpleasant duties and those whose sole aim was to be as awkward as possible. The latter, who were all objectors on the lowest of political grounds, referred to the others as the 'bloody purists' and did everything they could to make life miserable for them.

The position of the conscientious objector raises many of the most thorny questions not only of Church and State but also of the State and the individual. If a 'free society' is one in which differences are not merely tolerated but appreciated, to what extent may a difference be carried without involving action by the community? The countries of the world exhibit a variety of views in answer to this question. The position in Britain with regard both to war and to national service is that conscientious objectors state their case to a tribunal, and if it is accepted they are given alternative service, such as teaching, hospital attendance, gardening or manual or office work of some kind. These various activities are recognized by the community as equivalent in value to war service and so conscientious objection is so to speak given a political status parallel to the military status of a soldier. For

[1] See *The Communist Technique in Britain*, by Bob Darke (Penguin Special, 1952). Darke is a working man and a Hackney borough councillor and an ex-Communist. The case he presents shows the corruption of human life that takes place when a man becomes subservient to an iron discipline. The Communist party is not alone in this. It has been characteristic even of Christian Churches that have adopted the same attitude.

this reason no doubt many 'absolutists' object to alternative service altogether and during the First World War the proportion of such absolutists was far greater than in the second war when the position was standardized. A refusal to do any service whatsoever was frequently interpreted as a rejection of the common burden of citizenship and a claim to be the sole judge of one's duties as a member of the community. It was more a mark of the ideologist than of the man with genuine religious or even reasonable political convictions.

In some other countries no provision whatever has been made for alternative service. In Switzerland, for instance, a conscientious objector is treated exactly as any other lawbreaker, and for a country with a presumably democratic tradition (always excepting its attitude to women) its laws are particularly severe in this matter of military service. For this position, however, two arguments may be stated. First of all, if a man openly chooses to break the law he cannot feel aggrieved if he has to endure the consequences. His remedy is to seek to have the law altered. In Britain the situation was similar after the first introduction of conscription at a time when 'alternative service' was interpreted by most of the tribunals as 'alternative *military* service', i.e. with the Medical Corps or the Army Service Corps or some other presumably non-combatant branch of the services. The penalties imposed on those (and they were very many) who refused every form of military service and were tried by court martial were so severe that they shocked the public conscience into an alteration of the instructions to the military authorities. The climax came when ten young men were sent out to France and were ordered to be shot—a sentence which, however, was never carried out. But in neutral Switzerland men are imprisoned and if they still refuse military service they are imprisoned again. It would seem to be a very bad law that recognizes only one way of serving the community.

Secondly, it cannot be left to the individual to determine what is the proper attitude to take up with regard to the law. To some extent this would seem to be the case in Britain where tribunals (at any rate in peace-time) are usually sympathetic to cases of conscience. But carried to its logical conclusion this would be the end of all corporate action and indeed of law as an expression of the will of the community.

That liberty of individual action can be combined with obedience to the will of the group has, however, been the experience of the Society of Friends even in war-time. Obedience to the inward light is the characteristic tenet of Quakerism and this, of course, has at any rate the appearance of an exaltation of the Christian conscience of the individual over every other consideration. How then can this be operative during war service when somebody has to give orders concerning, say, the movement of a convoy and somebody else has got to obey them? What if the second person's 'inward light' tells him to do no such thing? In actual practice this does not happen, *not* because the second person submits to the first but because the second and the first and everybody else are under the same sense of concern for the cause. As Professor Roger Wilson puts it in a notable passage:

> Undertaking work 'under concern' means that the whole service is the Lord's and puts the Chairman, the General Secretary, the shorthand-typist, the lorry-driver, the storekeeper, the doctor and the accountant under an equal moral and spiritual commitment. And because, as we recognize in the whole of our Quaker method of meeting for worship and for discipline, there is equality before the Lord, so there was an equality of responsibility in Friends' Relief Service which invalidated all orthodox conceptions of executive relationships.[1]

It is evident from the work of the Friends' Relief Service that it is possible to give an adequate service to the community while still maintaining a witness against war and without setting up the isolated individual conscience as the sole rule of life. That conscience itself becomes regulated both by the corporate witness of the group and also by the overruling loyalty to the person and the mind of Christ—two safeguards against antinomianism.

It is when 'conscientious objection' drifts away from these two anchorages or refuses to accept them that it gets in the fairway of political and religious action. The objector may be violent and unyielding and ready to face the consequences, but that does not

[1] *Authority, Leadership and Concern* (Swarthmore Lecture, 1949), p. 35.

of itself make his position a matter of conscience. The issues which can be genuinely matters of conscience, matters, that is to say, which are so deeply integrated into a man's whole life that he would be denying himself and denying God if he gave way, are in my opinion very few indeed. Take, for instance, the case of 'conscientious objection' to vaccination. It is based sometimes on a belief that God has created the child perfect and to vaccinate him is an insult to the Creator. Sometimes it is based on the fact that some children have been made ill by vaccination. The second argument is one which is susceptible to statistics and if the balance of evidence is overwhelmingly on the side of vaccination (as it surely is) then it is wilful obstinacy rather than conscientious objection which is at the root of the refusal. As to the first argument the evidence again disposes, or ought to dispose, of it. The incredible fall in the figures of infantile mortality in the last fifty years, due to an improved medical and maternity service, indicates to any reasonable religious person that God requires man to co-operate with him in the working out of his purposes. In neither case can the objection to vaccination be considered as a position which involves a man's spiritual integrity.

The use of Sunday is a problem which has created a Church and State issue because of certain ancient Acts of Parliament that deal with it. It is worth noticing that regulations concerning the use of Sunday were by no means an invention of the Puritans. The eighth century saw the identification of the Christian Sunday with the Jewish Sabbath and an edict of Charlemagne in 789 forbade all Sunday labour. Church councils from this time onwards, and in the Catholic Church long after the Reformation, regulated Sunday behaviour, especially in the matter of games and dancing. In England in James I's reign the use of Sunday became a matter of keen controversy and the Book of Sports issued in 1618 allowed all sports save bull- and bear-baiting. Yet only seven years later an Act of Parliament forbade people to go out of their parishes on Sundays for the sake of amusement. An Act of 1677, in force till 1871, regulated Sunday trading and travelling, but by the later Act proceedings could be instituted against offenders only by obtaining the written consent of the Chief Constable. The Act whose survival has caused most criticism is that of 1781, by which any place of entertainment open on Sundays where a charge is made for admission might be deemed by the magistrates to be a 'disorderly house' and thereby liable to prosecution. Although for the most part this Act is a dead letter, it was until recently open to any informer to institute proceedings in accordance with the law.

The changed habits of the people, and the growth of towns and cities in contrast to the essentially village conditions of earlier centuries, the development of motor transport, and above all the effect of two world wars have made the State regulation of Sunday almost an anachronism. Building operations go on on Sundays, football matches, baseball and other sports take no account of days, and it is a cause of remark, either of surprise or of admiration, when an athlete loses the chance of a gold medal because he would not run on a Sunday. It is sometimes a matter of concern among good Protestants to notice the freedom the Catholic Church allows in these matters at a time when Sunday is becoming more and more 'secularized' and, according to the Lord's Day Observance Society, stands in need of 'defence'. Unfortunately 'defence' often means the use of obsolete Acts of Parliament to attempt to impose on our urbanized and highly complex society the habits and beliefs of an earlier village community. These matters are usually raised at the local level and the opening of cinemas and theatres on Sundays is left to the magistrates.

It would appear that what has been happening in our time has been the transformation of the Sunday question from a genuine matter of the Christian consciences (according to our definition) to a matter of ideology. The case for Sunday as a day of 'rest', i.e. cessation of ordinary work, is urged nowadays on the 'secular' grounds of health and refreshment, but this is not any longer an issue of Church and State. The one day off in the week is itself a valuable arrangement, but it is doubtful if this would ever have happened had not the Church earlier held it in trust, as it were, for later generations.

## 5 THE MYTH OF UNITY

It has just been pointed out that 'fraternity' itself can become an ideology. It can become a programme for the future instead of an attitude to be taken up here and now. In the religious world this is probably best illustrated by what might be called the 'myth' of unity.

When the divisions between individuals or churches or classes or nations have become so deep as to be both obvious and exasperating the idea of unity becomes charged with almost mystical significance. John Addington Symonds's hymn conveys just precisely this atmosphere. The sentiment becomes so powerful as almost to be an end in itself and to inhibit any practical steps being taken to implement it. Of recent years it has been noticeable in Church circles that the phrase 'our unhappy divisions' is found more often on the lips of those who do nothing at all to end them than of those who start off from the belief that all Christians are one in Christ. Accordingly there is set up this myth of unity not as a present underlying fact, but as that

> one far-off divine event
> To which the whole creation moves.

It is worth while, therefore, to analyse the factors in this curious situation in order to see if we cannot reassemble them in a more reasonable way.

First of all, unity and fraternity are by no means the same thing, and if they are alternatives the second is more to be preferred than the first. The desire for unity has as one of its roots the dislike that we all have of differences. We claim individuality for ourselves whether in the form of liberty or of equality, but it is by no means easy for us to allow other people a similar freedom, especially if their difference from us either gets in the way of our own self-expression or is a standing rebuke to our own ability or attitude. Consequently we do all we can to iron out differences by converting the other man to our own point of view. This is an element in that kind of propaganda the aim of which is to have everybody thinking or acting alike on some specific issue. It is a very subtle form of self-flattery and there are few people whose hearts are so pure as to be able to allow other people complete freedom to accept or to reject the policy put before them. Where persuasion fails and where coercion is possible, it plays up to the baser instincts of mankind to compel the other person to come in. The desire for unity is an extension of one's own self-regard, for even with the best will in the world it is almost impossible not to be piqued by other people's insistence on having a different point of view from our own.

Here then is one of the non-theological considerations that help to create a myth of unity. In these recent years there have been published a number of books from the Roman side of the reunion question, and some of them have shown not only a clear understanding of, but also a warm sympathy with, the Protestant position. But they all come back in the last resort to insistence on the full acceptance of the Roman position as the condition of unity. This is not a case for surprise, for ever since the Council of Trent four centuries ago there has been built up in the Roman Church a structure of exclusiveness and infallibility which would make it impossible to give way on one point without giving way on all. And here let it be said that there is a myth of infallibility as well as a myth of unity, with this difference, however, that while unity awaits achievement in the future infallibility within a closed circle can be acted upon at once. Some Protestants find this Roman claim an intolerable arrogance, but this is an exaggerated attitude. It is open to anyone to claim infallibility and on occasion most of us do so. What really matters is not who claims it but who concedes it, and if we find that it is conceded only by adherents to the particular group, whether Romanist or Plymouth Brethren or Jehovah's Witnesses, it need not be taken too seriously by those outside. It is indeed an inevitable consequence of strong conviction, and is to be found not only in churches and propaganda groups but also in commercial hotels and among football fans.

Secondly, in the matter of religion what do we mean by 'our unhappy divisions'? Is it the fact of division itself that is unhappy, or is it the attitude among the divided parts that is unhappy? This is a very real distinction, for it is possible to make out a good case in defence of our divisions while at the same time deploring our attitude to them.

There is indeed nothing more mythological in the whole range of the relations of Church and State than the use of the word 'unhappy' in reference to the denominations of Christendom. It is rarely if ever applied to one's own denomination, but usually to the others. Yet to view denominations in this light is to ignore a principle which is just as relevant in the ecclesiastical world as in the world of science or economics or any other worth-while sphere of human action. This is the principle of specialization. It is a mistake to view specialization as due to mere utilitarianism, to the fact that in the realm of knowledge we are beaten by quantity and must therefore limit ourselves to one particular section of the field. There is much more to it than that. In order to understand any organism we must see it both in its setting and out of its setting. There are sides of its life which never come into view as long as we consider it *only* in relationship to something else. And of course the reverse is also true. Both, therefore, are necessary. And to have a full-orbed view of the Christian life and of Christian society it has clearly been necessary to see the different aspects of Christianity both separate and together. Episcopacy represents one aspect, but Congregationalism represents another just as vital and just as capable of tracing its origin to the New Testament. The Christian life is seen in one aspect as activity, as meditation it is seen in another, and as scholarship in another. To some men religion is a matter of knowledge, to others of emotion, to others of choice, to others of action and to others of 'belonging'. All are necessary and it is quite gratuitous for the representatives of one type of witness to assume that their particular witness must be regulative of the whole. It is because this has happened in the past that those who have come to new experience and who have found a new witness to uphold have had to break away from the majority group and develop their own particular witness in isolation.

Of course there have also been present many other non-theological factors—the desire for power, local class-distinctions, racial prejudice (as between the French and the Germans in the 'undivided' Church of the Middle Ages), and other unamiable influences. Nevertheless the divisions have not all been due to superfluity of naughtiness on the part of those who have come out, although they have very often been the fault of those who stayed in, but many of them have arisen through the clear guidance of the spirit of God. The proof of this has been that the special witness that they have cherished and developed has been something for the good of the whole Church. Who nowadays ever thinks of John Bunyan as simply a Baptist minister or of David Livingstone as a Congregationalist missionary? It comes as a shock to realize that Livingstone would probably have been refused Communion by the missionaries of the Universities' Mission to Central Africa which was founded as a result of his appeal! When recently celebrations were held at a Lincolnshire town in honour of the Pilgrim Fathers it was in the very parish church from which they had been driven out. The ministry of silent worship which was developed by the Society of Friends is nowadays valued by every type of church. The witness of the Anglo-Catholic section of the Church of England to a more spiritual view of the Church and an orderly form of worship has been taken up within the Free Churches and is now part of the witness of all the churches. No copyright is possible in the things that are of God. If the fruits of the Spirit are made manifest by any group, however small or however large, they become part of the heritage of the whole Church.

Separatism is as necessary to the well-being of a community as ecumenicity. The Roman Church well understands this fact. Given the acceptance of the fundamental principle of the infallibility of the Pope and the authority of the Church it is astonishing what a variety of organization within the organization is permitted. It has already been noted[1] that on the Congo mission field in 1937 seventy-nine separate Roman Catholic missions were at work.

[1] Above, p. 32.

There is a proliferation of orders and communities, and this satisfies at one and the same time the human impulse to belong to a group larger than oneself and also to have freedom to be oneself. The only condition, of course, is the necessary acceptance of the fundamental principle, and it is this which prevents any radical reformation of the Roman Church from within.[1] To deny the major principle has meant of necessity total separation and the development of a Christian witness elsewhere.

Within Protestantism the myth of unity has taken various forms. There are those who are attracted by the splendid isolation of the Roman Church, its assurance, its continuity and its internationalism. They long for union with the ancient Church, but as the ancient Church has no intention of lowering its conditions of admission and has indeed in the last ten years made them even stiffer than before, and as these Protestant fellow travellers are finally unwilling to accept the conditions, the myth of unity remains a myth and can never be anything else. On the other hand the Anglo-Catholic party has itself no intention of lowering its conditions of union with the Free Churches, so it is in the curious position of claiming equality with Rome, which Rome refuses to grant, and at the same time itself refusing to grant equality to the Free Churches. The words 'sect' and 'separatist' would seem therefore to adhere more realistically to those who exclude from fellowship rather than to those who are excluded. The size of the group concerned is not a relevant factor at all for in this specific situation there is nothing to choose between a strict Baptist Church and the Church of Rome. Both cherish a doctrine of infallibility, and both act on the principle of unchurching those who disagree with them. That eminent Roman Catholic layman, Baron von Hügel, drew a distinction between the ancient Catholic Church and the Roman Church after the Council of Trent and gave the impression in conversation that in certain ways—not in all—the later Roman Church conformed more closely to Troeltsch's

[1] A Catholic writer, W. Teeling, *The Pope in Politics* (1937), has an interesting section on the relations of the Vatican with the Catholic Bishops of the United States which illustrates this point (chapter 15).

description of a sect than to that of a church. And if this could be said with even partial truth of the Roman Catholic Church it must be still more true of that party in the Church of England which uses or misuses the adjective 'catholic'.

Nevertheless the Anglo-Catholic party has succeeded in imposing upon the Church of England its own ideals as the orthodox structure of unity. It includes episcopacy as the channel of grace and not simply as the mode of organization. (In this latter sense all the larger Free Churches are already developing episcopacy under their own special terminology.) It requires episcopal confirmation as the condition of partaking of Communion—an act which is itself 'celebrated' or performed by an episcopally ordained priest and is not merely a celebration of some other event. This ordination and this confirmation as well as baptism are physical acts which are believed to impart a spiritual grace. The intention is not enough without the physical act itself, and full church membership therefore is dependent upon the undergoing of this particular rite of confirmation. The acceptance also of an ancient creed as the 'sufficient statement' of faith and the condition of membership is also required, and 'the Holy Scriptures as the record of God's revelation of himself to man' as the 'rule and ultimate standard of faith'. These four points—the ministry, the creeds, the sacraments and the Bible—are what is known as the 'Lambeth Quadrilateral' and were laid down in 1884 as the basis on which reunion might be sought.

The larger Free Churches of England and the non-episcopal churches of America contain groups that might be willing to accept the Anglo-Catholic conditions and are concerned to use propaganda in their own churches in that direction. All these movements, however, the Anglican towards Rome and the non-episcopal towards what is called Catholicism, are part of the myth of unity which has taken so strong a hold upon Christian people of recent years. It is called a myth not because it is unreal or illusory but because it ignores the very solid facts which are present in all human association. It is also a myth because, unlike the development of Christianity (and also unlike the development of

English law), it begins with an idea or an ideology and seeks to apply that to the situation instead of dealing with practical issues first and being content to discover new principles as we go along. The Anglo-Catholic view of God and the world cannot be taken as the goal of all ecumenical endeavour. What that goal is we do not yet know but the way to it begins with fraternity. To set up an ideal constructed out of present prejudices, allowing for no development in the future, is to act on a myth instead of on reality.

Accordingly, if we believe in the fatherhood of God and that all men are brothers, let us see what this means in a given situation. A small Yorkshire village has in it a parish church and two chapels. The population of the village is 2000 and the total church-going population less than 200. In that village, brotherhood among Christians has nothing at all to do with the Lambeth Quadrilateral. It has a great deal to do with the goodwill that exists between the vicar and the Free Church people (there is no resident minister in the village). Does he welcome them to his church? Is he willing on occasion to go to their churches? Any rules he may have about Holy Communion will not distress them for they would not want to attend in any case, but an exhibition of social snobbery would distress them very much. Fortunately, however, the vicar is completely friendly and lends a hand to both the chapels when they need it. In a Cambridgeshire village during the illness of the Baptist minister the High Church rector, who wore a biretta, sent his curate across to the chapel to take the services for them! The present vicar of a church in Cambridge similarly took charge of the Congregational church in his former Bristol parish during a vacancy. In another Cambridgeshire village during a confirmation the bishop and clergy robed in the Congregational schoolroom and the whole Free Church population turned out to support their vicar. This is the kind of unity that is not mythological and is in marked contrast to the attitude of a vicar in another county who gave each little Anglican boy scout half a crown to stay away from a scouts' parade in the Congregational chapel! It is the personal relationship between local groups that is the important thing.

Whatever goes on at Lambeth or Memorial Hall is the concern of quite a different set of people from those in the villages and towns. The Free Churches have complete freedom of exchange between their ministers, and the Lord's Supper is open to all who desire to come—the obligation is on the believer and not on the presiding officer. The fact that they worship in different buildings in the same neighbourhood is regrettable, but it is not the 'scandal' that some people would make of it. The only scandal in church relations is unbrotherliness and it is to be found here and there on the side of the Church of England and here and there on the Free Church side. The existence of Roman Catholics does not affect the issue one way or another any more than does the existence of, say, a Masonic temple. Their position is well known and the 'scandal', if there be a scandal, is not because of Catholic versus Protestant but because of lack of fraternity among Protestants.

But the establishment of the Anglican Church as the Church of the nation creates a moral obligation that it should behave as such. A keynote of the Church of England has been comprehension, and although it would be impossible nowadays to revive the arrant Erastianism of the days before the Oxford Movement it is morally even if not theologically reprehensible for the pulpits of parish churches and cathedrals to be closed to all Christian Englishmen save those of a particular theological affiliation while they are open to foreigners 'in communion' with the Anglican church. No responsible Free Churchman nowadays would wish for disestablishment, for the Free Church grievance is not against the establishment as such but against his national heritage being treated simply as a denominational asset. It is this lack of fraternity that is the real offence. If the Church of England were alive to its opportunities it could very soon become the church of the whole nation in fact as well as in theory. But so long as this sectarian attitude persists, there will be need for the Free Church witness as something entirely separate. It is a matter of profound regret that in hundreds of parishes in rural England village life is split in two by the intransigence of the parish church. The attachment of villagers for their parish church is strong even among Nonconformists, and they quite often like to be married in church. Yet it may happen that they are forbidden because of their religious persuasion, and a theological position is made to serve as an excuse for the exercise of power. The parish as a whole, however, takes a quiet revenge, for the men who take such an attitude lose their position of leadership. When men try to be 'fathers' without being brothers they lose their claim even while asserting it.

## 6 INTERNATIONAL FRATERNITY

On the international scale the question of fraternity is the biggest issue of all. In the absence of fraternity men go to war or they stir up the passions that ultimately lead to war. Outside the Roman and the Orthodox Churches there is no church nowadays that would affirm that war could ever be Christian. It may have to be waged as the only means left to defend a Christian civilization, but the fact that it is so indicates a failure of Christian brotherhood at an earlier stage. The difficulty about pacifism, however, is that it is not only an affirmation about the wrongness of war but also a suggested method of dealing with it. It is as if, when a man is at death's door, we were to suggest a cure for cancer which might have been effective if applied earlier. The Christian attitude to other people is not something to be suddenly applied when a crisis has arisen, but a way of life which would prevent the crisis arising at all. The effectiveness of pacifism as a method of dealing with war depends upon two considerations—the time when it is applied and the measure of unanimity which lies behind it. It has been said, for instance, by Dr Donald Soper, that if England were to stand aside and refuse to defend herself against invasion one of two things would happen. Either such a quantity of spiritual power would thereby be released that no invader could stand against it, or it would become a martyr nation whose martyrdom would have atoning value in international relations in days to come. Without passing any judgement on the highly hypothetical nature of these consequences we might call in question the formulation of the major premise. What exactly do we mean by 'England' in this context? Does it mean the Cabinet or the Government or the electorate? And if it means even a majority of any of these has the majority the right to offer up as a sacrifice even a single dissentient? It has always been held that the remark of Caiaphas 'that it was expedient that one man should die for the people' represented a thoroughly pagan attitude. Whatever conduct a man may feel to be in accordance with his own idealism he can hardly expect people who do not share those ideals to act as if they did.

This of course is not the only aspect of pacifism. Apart altogether from the discussion of national policy there remains the question of individual action. Whether a person should fight or not, should be willing to kill or not, is a personal matter to be settled by his own conscience. It is in reality quite a different issue. But to make it a genuine matter of conscience, there needs to be some consistency between a man's attitude to his fellows long before and during the crisis and his present witness. Some pacifists are anything but pacific and the determination not to be killed oneself is often rationalized into a concern for high ideals.

The establishment of brotherhood among the nations is beset by difficulties which arise from the fact that we are here dealing with groups that are by no means homogeneous. Indeed this is true of every large group, not only nations but churches, trade unions and schools. It was one of the fallacious arguments used against woman suffrage that what was called the 'women's vote' might be the deciding factor in many elections. The assumption here was that all women would vote exactly alike, just as it is assumed that all the people in a nation will act exactly alike. The unwillingness to see within other nations the variety and the distinctions that are in one's own nation has been a not uncommon cause of war. Fraternity among nations will be delayed so long as we look upon a nation as an undifferentiated unit. The Hegelian view of the State as a corporate community with a soul of its own not only has been used to justify aggression and violence but it is in itself a complete obstacle to fraternity. For fraternity is a matter of personal concern on both sides and is not a product of organization. It is a sentiment which cuts across all natural and class barriers and is indeed a new type of alignment. The Marxian slogan 'Workers of the world unite, you have nothing to lose but your chains' recognizes a similar horizontal way of dividing up the peoples of the world as distinct from the vertical national divisions, but it suffers from the same fallacy that besets nationalism. It assumes that all workers will think and act alike and that they all recognize the same fundamental common characteristic—that they are all held in thraldom and what is required to bring them together is organization. If we are to have slogans at all to express our universal fraternity there is none more relevant than the remark of George Fox: 'Speak to that which is of God in every man'. The link here is with man as man, not man as worker or Englishman or scholar, but simply man as a child of God.

Professor Arnold Toynbee has certain delusions of his own. He would like a super-state to which all the various states of the world would render homage—a sort of fulfilment on the international scale of what Hobbes supposed to have happened in the history of the individual state. All nations would lay aside their sovereignty and enter into some sort of social contract which would be the end of war. This is the medieval myth of unity returned. The link in the Middle Ages in the West was the Catholic Church, but it was more apparent than real. It was an organization based on an apparently common Christian faith, but quite unable to prevent race conflicts between Latins and Teutons and also unable to tame the savage passions of men. Fear was its only sanction and the idea of brotherhood was entirely absent. Even law was local and national and the conflict of laws, which was frequent during international fairs, could be solved only by reliance on common sense. Just as no juggling with money can guarantee equality and no limiting of government interference can guarantee liberty, so no manipulation of organization can guarantee fraternity. Indeed this approaches the question from the wrong end. It has already been pointed out that whereas fraternity is to the politicians and social reformers a goal in the future the essentially Christian attitude is that it is here now and requires to be acted upon. All the organizations for international brotherhood start off with the assumption that men are enemies and have got to be turned into friends, rather than that in the sight of God they are friends and need to make real that friendship.

The difference between the two points of view is made clear when we look at the organization of the United Nations or at the League of Nations which preceded it. As we have seen, Professor H. A. Smith has pointed out[1] that in both cases the rightness or wrongness of a war was made to turn upon procedure. If one belligerent had given due notice within the prescribed formula and the other had neglected to do so, then the case of the first was held to be justified. Yet even this procedure is crossed by another which depends on the size and power of the parties concerned. Over the Suez crisis of 1957 Israel apparently followed the prescribed procedure rather than Egypt. On the Hungarian issue Russia was demonstrably in the wrong. But sanctions were threatened against Israel and not against Russia.

Fraternity, therefore, cannot be produced by machinery. It can come only through the recognition of a sincere appreciation of one another. I have used this expression rather than to say 'a common faith' because 'a common faith' may itself be no more than an external conformity and a form of organization. We have tried that sort of thing before in Europe and it has failed. I therefore see no hope for the world in what is often looked upon as the reunion of the scattered parts of Christendom, not even when it is given a metaphysical flavour as the re-weaving of the seamless robe of Christ. Separateness in organization is neither good nor bad. It can be either, and it can be convenient. But separation in spirit and in personal regard is a very serious thing and the solution of it takes precedence over every other type of concern.

Some forty years ago I attended an International Students' Congress in Prague. It was very soon after World War I and the younger representatives of the nations had been called together

[1] Above, p. 46.

to see how they could build a new world. The atmosphere was almost solid with suspicion. The different groups were constantly trying to outmanœuvre one another. Meetings were prolonged by one group until from very weariness members of an opposing group went home to bed, only to find next morning that in their absence resolutions had been passed to which they could by no means agree. Propaganda was shrill and continuous, and apart from the social events there seemed to be no point in having the gathering at all.

In the middle of all this a notice was put up inviting all members of the various Student Christian Movements to a tea party. They came and they were addressed by Miss Ruth Rouse. Every nation that was represented in the larger gathering was represented in this gathering, but whereas the conference as a whole could achieve no effective bond of union the smaller group had it ready to hand and the feeling was most cordial.

In a free society, nations, races, denominations, and other groups will continue to exist. This is a condition of liberty. And in so far as each appreciates the others and accepts the fact of difference there will be equality. But none of this is possible without as a basis the pragmatic activity of that spiritual principle of brotherhood. This is the Church's task in the world—not to make converts to a creed or to accept a common organization, but to provide an area within which the fatherhood of God is operative as a way of life. I confess that I see no way of doing this without the Christian religion. There is brotherhood in Buddhism, in Hinduism and above all in Islam, but it is in every case on a limited basis. To say that all religions accept the fatherhood of God as a principle may get us no further than to sign our name in acceptance of the Nicene Creed. Whatever is ultimately meant by 'the grace of our Lord Jesus Christ' either in the New Testament or in familiar usage, it has always been an experience down the ages that in some mysterious fashion the Christian way of life is more than a way but brings with it an access of power to perform that which we in our hearts of hearts desire. There is enough theoretical good will in the world. There is much talk of humanity. But there is little compassion, little sympathy, and little of that stern disciplining of oneself for the sake of the human family. It is this rather than a new theory or a new organization that the world most desperately needs.

Here then ends this brief outline of the factors that arise in a free society in the relations of Church and State. If we look beyond the Church simply as an institution and the State simply as the Government we can see that the ideal pattern for society is that of a human family in which old and young, male and female, can live together with all the differences in temperament, ability and vocation appreciated by each other and hence equal in the sight of God and of themselves. It is the function of the Church to keep alive and cherish that spirit of fraternity which is the very basis of a free society.

And to sum up in one sentence the thesis of this book we may take the oft-quoted remark of Bishop Berkeley:

> Whatever the world thinks, he who hath not meditated upon God, the human mind, and the *summum bonum*, may possibly make a thriving earthworm, but will most indubitably make a sorry patriot and a sorry statesman.

APPENDIX I

# THE WORD 'CATHOLIC'

The adjective in its derivation has no ecclesiastical significance at all. It simply means 'general', 'widespread', 'in common use'. As such it appears in Ignatius, who defines 'catholicity' as 'wherever Jesus Christ is'—a phrase capable of much confusion. Later Cyril of Jerusalem mentions four marks of universality: widespread as opposed to local, complete in doctrine, applicable to all men and concerned with all virtues. It appears in this sense in the Nicene Creed, while the Edict of Milan uses only the term 'Christian'. It is clear that the ecclesiastics continually used it in the sense of 'the majority' and as such it appears for the first time in an official publication in the edict of Theodosius II in 380. Here it is plainly a party term, and henceforth was always used as such. The edict defines Christianity as that doctrine followed by Pope Damasus and Peter, Bishop of Alexandria, and continues: 'We authorize those who follow this doctrine to receive the title "Catholic Christian", but others we judge to be mad and raving and worthy of incurring the disgrace of heretical teaching, nor are their assemblies to receive the name of churches. They are to be punished not only by Divine retribution but also by our own action.'[1] The Latin text will be found in Harnack's *History of Dogma*, IV, p. 94, note. Harnack's comment is: 'It is in the highest degree characteristic of his [i.e. Theodosius'] whole policy that this faith is more definitely described as the Roman and Alexandrian faith, i.e. the new doctrinal orthodoxy of Cappadocia and Asia is passed over in silence.' In other words, the term 'catholic' was a party term and indicated that party which the State would henceforth support, while the minority could expect the physical force of the emperor to be used against them.

[1] Ehler and Morrall, *Church and State through the Centuries* (Burns and Oates, 1954), p. 7.

APPENDIX II

# THE CASE OF THE BISHOP OF PRATO

While this book was passing through the press there arose in Italy a *cause célèbre* which brought into the clearest relief the Roman Catholic position on Church and State.

Since the Council of Trent (1563) the Catholic Church had required of Italians an ecclesiastical ceremony in order to validate a marriage. This was to be followed or preceded by a civil ceremony in order to satisfy the legal requirements of the State. But by the Concordat which Mussolini made with the Vatican in 1929 the religious ceremony conducted according to Canon Law became of itself sufficient to ensure the 'civil effects' of the marriage, and a purely civil ceremony was now no longer necessary. Most Italians in practice have been satisfied with this one ceremony in church but the Concordat did not invalidate in the eyes of the law a marriage celebrated with civil rites only. Mussolini indeed explicitly stated that the Concordat was intended to allow those who did not want a religious ceremony to have the civil ceremony alone. Nevertheless, as if to neutralize this permission, the Sacred Congregation of the Discipline of the Sacraments almost immediately afterwards issued an instruction to the priests to see to it that Catholics were duly married with religious rites and to declare that any who were married by civil rites only were to be treated as public sinners.

Apparently in the diocese of Prato there had been an increasing number of civil marriages and the bishop (Mgr Fiordelli) at last felt that the time had come to make a public example. He chose for this purpose a young grocer of Prato, Signor Mauro Bellandi, a well-known Communist who had long since ceased to practise as a Catholic and had been married to Signorina Loriana Nunziati by the Communist mayor of Prato. In a pastoral letter the bishop denounced these young people by name, declared them to be public sinners living 'in scandalous concubinage', ordered that they should be denied the Sacraments, that their house should not be blessed, and that Signorina Nunziati's parents, for permitting this 'immensely sinful and scandalous step', should be denied holy water at Easter. The marriage was held to be no marriage at all.

Bellandi took all this as a slander on his and his wife's character and when business began to fall off at his store and he began to get abusive anonymous letters he sued the bishop and his priest in the civil court in Florence for libel and slander. Fiordelli was the first bishop to be arraigned before an Italian court since the Concordat of 1929.

The bishop refused to attend, on the ground that no civil court had jurisdiction over him when acting in his spiritual capacity. He argued that to appear in court would be an acknowledgement that a civil magistrate could adjudicate on 'an act regarding the spiritual government of the faithful'. At this a national controversy flared up. It was particularly bitter, of course, in the Left-wing newspapers, but even the *Corriere della Sera*, the Conservative newspaper of Milan, declared that once the principle of the supremacy of the Canon Law over the law of the land were admitted the entire clergy would become a privileged class exempt from the law that applied to ordinary citizens.

The trial began in Florence on 24 February 1958 without the bishop, and his lawyers argued that there was a difference between a civil reputation and a religious one and that the bishop had been concerned only with Bellandi's religious reputation—a form of hair-splitting which Bellandi's lawyers indignantly disowned. The judges moreover were not impressed, and while they acquitted the priest as only an agent they found the bishop guilty of criminal defamation. He was fined 40,000 lire and ordered to pay damages and costs. The Left-wing paper *Avanti* hailed this as a victory for liberty and held that the sentence proved that in Italy all are equal before the law. With this many Italians of other political persuasions were in agreement. But all the churches in the Archdiocese of Bologna went into mourning and were ordered to sound a funeral peal each day until Palm Sunday. The Pope cancelled the celebration of the nineteenth anniversary of his coronation because of the 'bitterness, grief and outrage' suffered by the Church from the verdict of an Italian court. The bishop's own comment, according to the reporter of the American magazine *Time*, was 'I am serene. Remember that Jesus Christ died on the Cross.'

# INDEX